What people are s

The Medium and the Minister

This book provides a carefully considered balance between a religious and non-religious view of the afterlife. It is well written and provides compelling evidence for such a proposition. The author has included many excellent evidential examples which would be hard to dispute. He is a fastidious researcher and has a compelling and enjoyable style of writing. I am sure that you will be enthralled by this book and it will be up to you to digest the information provided and come to your own conclusions, while maintaining an open mind on these matters.
Tricia J. Robertson, researcher and author of *Things You Can Do When You're Dead!*, *More Things You Can Do When You're Dead* and *It's Life and Death, But Not As You Know It!*

Roger Straughan has written an erudite but accessible book on the eternal question of life after death. He examines how the subject has been tackled by both scientists and theologians, placing these apparently disparate approaches into their proper historical context, whilst at the same time shedding new light on how various experts in the field have tackled the subject of the afterlife. He is a well-respected researcher and author who has the knowledge and expertise to guide the reader through this fascinating subject. The approach he takes makes this a unique and thoroughly absorbing book.
David Taylor, researcher, editor of *Psychical Studies* and Secretary of the Unitarian Society for Psychical Studies

Roger Straughan is a philosopher and writer on paranormal topics. He is, therefore, very well qualified to write on these matters. He brings to them his characteristic balance and lucidity.

What stands out is his sensitivity and understanding of both perspectives: that of the Christian and the psychical researcher. In the process of exploring these viewpoints he reassesses the reputation and achievements of Sir Arthur Conan Doyle and Sir Oliver Lodge who have sometimes been unfairly portrayed in the media and historical texts. His book is especially valuable in that he brings into one place and makes coherent the rather tortured relationship with spiritualistic phenomena that the Anglican Church has displayed over the years. The book is a refreshingly well-written and accessible exploration of this topic.

Trevor Hamilton, MA, PhD, author of *Immortal Longings: FWH Myers and the Victorian Search for Life After Death* and *Arthur Balfour's Ghosts: An Edwardian Elite and the Riddle of the Cross-Correspondence Automatic Writings*

The Medium
and the Minister

Who on Earth Knows about the Afterlife?

The Medium and the Minister

Who on Earth Knows about the Afterlife?

Roger Straughan

6TH
BOOKS

Winchester, UK
Washington, USA

JOHN HUNT PUBLISHING

First published by Sixth Books, 2022
Sixth Books is an imprint of John Hunt Publishing Ltd., No. 3 East St., Alresford,
Hampshire SO24 9EE, UK
office@jhpbooks.com
www.johnhuntpublishing.com
www.6th-books.com

For distributor details and how to order please visit the 'Ordering' section on our website.

ISBN: 978 1 78904 880 3
978 1 78904 881 0 (ebook)
Library of Congress Control Number: 2021932921

A CIP catalogue record for this book is available from the British Library.

Design: Stuart Davies

UK: Printed and bound by CPI Group (UK) Ltd, Croydon, CR0 4YY
Printed in North America by CPI GPS partners

We operate a distinctive and ethical publishing philosophy in
all areas of our business, from our global network of authors to
production and worldwide distribution.

Contents

Previous Titles

With O-Books:
A Study in Survival: Conan Doyle Solves the Final Problem
ISBN: 978-1-84694-240-2

With other publishers, titles include:

Beliefs, Behaviour and Education
Cassell, ISBN: 0-304-31860-4

*Can We Teach Children To Be Good? Basic Issues In Moral, Personal
and Social Education*
Open University Press, ISBN: 0-335-09524-0

Philosophizing About Education, coauthor with John Wilson
Holt, ISBN: 0-03-910430-3

Improving Nature? The Science and Ethics of Genetic Engineering,
coauthor with Michael Reiss
Cambridge University Press, ISBN: 0-521-63754-6
(several editions and translations)

Dedication

To the two knights and all seekers who have followed in their footsteps.

Introduction

Do you believe in life after death? Most people, if faced with this question, would probably not give just a straight yes-or-no answer, but would qualify or explain their reply in some way. For example, they might say one of the following:

1.   No, I'm not religious.
2.   Yes, I'm a Christian.
3.   No, I only believe what scientists can prove.
4.   Yes, I've looked at some of the evidence from psychical research.
5.   No, it's obvious that when you're dead, you're dead.
6.   Yes, I've seen lots of TV programs about mediums and near-death experiences.
7.   No, no one can ever know, so why bother about it?
8.   I'm not interested. It's this life that matters.

All of these responses raise many further questions, and this book will try to tackle some of these. My aim is not to provide conclusive answers (which is probably impossible, anyway), but rather to look at some of the arguments and assumptions surrounding the possibility of life after death to help you, the reader, to make up your own mind. This will inevitably take us into highly controversial areas and introduce us to a number of colorful personalities, because this subject has the potential to arouse strong passions and prejudices by challenging deeply-held beliefs.

One particular source of conflict has often centered on the role of religion here and the extent to which religious doctrines can offer satisfactory answers to those trying to work out what (if anything) it's reasonable to believe about a possible afterlife. This conflict will be examined in some detail in this book, because its origins highlight basic issues and attitudes which are still very much in evidence today. In fact, the idea for this book first came to me when I was signing copies at a local bookshop of a previous book about evidence for survival of death. One shopper took one look at the cover and exclaimed loudly, "I'm not interested in that. I'm a Christian!" before rushing out of the door – presumably to avoid spiritual pollution!

But religion doesn't have a monopoly over life-after-death issues. Nor is there a complete overlap between those who would call themselves 'religious' and those who believe in some form of post-mortem existence. As we shall see in Chapter 2, many 'non-religious' people would not subscribe to the view that death is the end, while many 'religious' people today (strangely perhaps) would be doubtful about any idea of an afterlife. So where else can we look for evidence and arguments for or against this belief?

Psychical researchers, or parapsychologists as they are now often labelled, have a long history of investigating the question and have accumulated a mountain of relevant data, which has generated radical disagreements over how it should be interpreted. Spiritualists on the other hand are convinced that their experiences of apparent communication with the 'dead' clearly demonstrate that personality survives. Some philosophers have tried to tackle the question of whether the existence of such a personality without a physical body is conceivable, while some psychologists have studied whether our minds, and therefore our consciousness, really are dependent upon our physical brains. Some scientists have even tried to examine the possible implications of quantum theory for this area.

It's probably fair to say that the vast majority of the general public are unaware of all this, or at least uninterested in it, as it seems to have little or no relevance to their everyday lives. They would be the most likely to reply to the question posed above along the lines of the last two answers, "Why bother? We can't really know for sure, so let's get on with this life." So are they right? Does it matter whether one believes in life after death? What difference does it make to anything?

We need to decide whether they are right or not at the outset, because if they are, I've wasted my time in writing this book and you will be wasting yours in reading it! So let's start with that challenge, before we attempt to explore this complex but fascinating question of what on earth can we know about a possible life after death.

Chapter 1

Why Bother About an Afterlife?

On the face of it, this sounds a very reasonable response to our initial question. Surely it's this life that matters, not some possible so-called afterlife, which may or may not exist and which we can't know anything about. Isn't it life before death that we should focus on, not some possible life after death? Shouldn't we concentrate on making this world and our life in it as good as we can and leave the next world to look after itself?

Certainly we can all agree that we should not become so preoccupied with the question of life after death that we switch off from this world and fail to play a full part in it. Life is for living – we have a life to live here and now, and we should make the most of it. But if we grant that obvious point, it doesn't follow that what may or may not follow this life doesn't matter at all, and that we shouldn't spend any time ever thinking about it. One of the very few things we can be absolutely certain of in this life is that it's going to end. We're all going to die someday sooner or later, and so it's not ridiculous to speculate occasionally about whether we might survive that inevitable physical death in some way.

Of course, it's a cliché nowadays to say that death is a taboo subject. Most people don't want to think or talk about it. Even many clergy don't want to talk about it, perhaps because some surveys show that a substantial number of them don't actually believe in life after death; most are certainly ill-informed about the subject and totally ignorant of the evidence, which is almost as odd as the idea of a solicitor [lawyer] unashamedly knowing nothing about the law. But thinking seriously about the possibility of an afterlife, whatever our conclusions, can at least help us to overcome that taboo and face the inevitable fact that we will all die one day. It helps us to make up our minds on this fundamental issue and not just accept the taboo by brushing the whole subject under the carpet.

Anyone prepared to consider the possibility of life after death is faced with a fundamental choice: between a materialistic view of life and one which allows for the possibility of some form of spiritual dimension beyond the known limits of the physical world. That choice is a very stark one. Are we just a random cocktail of chemicals and atoms, destined to disintegrate when the cells of our bodies and brains die? If so, it must follow that when you're dead you're dead, and that's all there is to it. Our life must then be, as Shakespeare memorably put it, "a tale told by an idiot, full of sound and fury, signifying nothing." Or is it conceivable that we might be something more permanent than that, something that has the capacity for survival and further development? Could this life be part of a bigger picture which we can at present get only brief and disjointed glimpses of? Which one of these two options we choose to accept cannot help but form part of our whole view of the world. That view includes our attitude towards others and ourselves, which in turn must shape the kind of person we become and the ways we behave.

One way to illustrate this is to consider how we react to news stories. The so-called 'taboo' about death doesn't seem to extend to these. Newspapers and TV news programs are heavily dependent on death and would have huge gaps to fill without it. How often do we hear and see news headlines dealing with murders, wars, massacres, natural disasters and fatal accidents? An obvious example here would be the domination of the media by the COVID-19 pandemic. If one reflects a little, it seems strange that death should be considered so 'newsworthy', as there is nothing 'new' about it or surprising that people regularly die in all sorts of ways. For light relief from these headlines we are often presented with reports of the latest 'miracle cure' for cancer or heart disease or the prospect of a vaccine for coronavirus, but these are deemed 'news' only because they may delay future deaths. The assumption behind all this is that death is the ultimate disaster, the worst thing that can conceivably happen: how awful that loss of life should occur! Politicians in the UK during the pandemic repeatedly emphasized that "every death is a tragedy".

Now of course no one would deny that our personal experience of the deaths of family members, friends and loved ones can often be shattering, because of the overwhelming sense of loss and shock we can feel at such times. But our reaction to such loss must be influenced to some extent by whether or not we believe that death equals total extinction. If we believe that it does, then dying really is the end of everything and the persons who have died have lost everything; they can no longer fulfil any purposes, achieve any goals or satisfy any desires. "How unfair!" is the frequent comment, "They didn't deserve to die!" The unspoken implication here is that dying is some sort of unmerited, final punishment, though few who make such comments pursue the question of who or what inflicts this punishment and why it is "unfair".

On the other hand, if we believe that death may not be the end and that personality may in some way survive, the sense of loss may be just as great, but it is mainly **our** loss and feelings of separation that are causing our sorrow for the death of loved ones, rather than pity for the person who has died. In the case of news reports of the deaths of total strangers (in war or natural disasters, for example), there can be no such sense of personal loss, and feelings of sorrow and pity can only really make sense if we believe that death does mean ultimate extinction.

Our beliefs about our own inevitable death must have an even greater effect upon our approach to life. Am I merely, as the materialist puts it, "four buckets of water and a bagful of salts"? If I believe that I am, what implications does that have for how I live my life? I may seek to avoid the prospect of my extinction by refusing to think or talk about it and become uncomfortable if the subject arises. I may become a hypochondriac, fearful of any possible signs of a lethal disease, or I may try to make arrangements to have my body frozen and preserved after death in the hope of being revived at some far-off future date. Alternatively, I may decide (consciously or subconsciously) that the only logical policy is to live in such a way as to maximize my own happiness and satisfaction, though how exactly I would set about achieving this is far from obvious and calls for considerable self-knowledge. (I may even find myself wondering how an accidental concoction of chemicals could manage to analyze itself!)

There are good reasons, then, why we should consider whether or not we believe there is some form of life after death. Many indeed have argued that this is the most important question that we can ask. Frederic Myers, for example, the eminent psychologist, poet, philosopher and psychical pioneer, whom we shall meet again later in this book, wrote at the beginning of his groundbreaking study *Human Personality* (1903): "The question for man most momentous of all is whether or not his personality involves any element which can survive bodily death. In this direction have always lain the greatest fears, the farthest-reaching hopes, which could either oppress or stimulate mortal minds."

Similarly, Dr. Raynor Johnson, a physicist, psychologist and researcher into psychical and mystical experience, firmly declared: "I can think of no question to which a clear and unequivocal answer is more important for human beings than the one 'Do the dead live?' A widespread conviction of this truth, as distinct from faith, hope, or agnosticism about it, would do more in my opinion to raise standards of conduct, to check materialism, and to lighten the valley of the shadow than the answer to any other single question." (1957)

The Cambridge philosopher, C.D. Broad, maintained that survival of death is "a necessary condition if the life of humanity is to be more than a rather second-rate farce." (1953)

But even if we are prepared to grant the importance of the question, it does still remain a question. **Do** we survive death? **Is** there an afterlife? The variety of possible answers offered in our Introduction shows that it's not at all obvious how we can set about tackling the question. One point that needs emphasizing at the outset is that it's a mistake to think in terms of possible 'proof' here, if by 'proof' we mean 100% guaranteed certainty. In fact, that degree of certainty isn't possible anywhere. I can't be 100% certain that I'm sitting at my computer at this moment and not in the middle of a dream or experiencing a hallucination. There's no certain proof that the sun will rise in the East and sink in the West tomorrow; some cataclysmic event may intervene and reverse the process. Unshakeable 'proof' doesn't exist within experimental science, as there's always the possibility of later experiments and findings overturning the provisional results of earlier ones. Even in Mathematics, the fundamental concepts and theories on which the whole of science and technology are based don't rest upon unassailable 'truths' which have been 'proved'. On a more practical level, verdicts are reached and accepted in criminal courts of law on the basis not of absolute 'proof', but of reasonable probability as presented by the evidence.

Of course, in our everyday lives we have to proceed on the assumption that many things **can** be relied upon to be true and have been 'proved' to be highly probable. Otherwise we would live in a state of permanent doubt and paralysis. It is 99.999% probable that many of the beliefs we take for granted (such as the sun rising in the East tomorrow) are true, but we should remember that we are always dealing with probabilities and not guaranteed proof.

So in considering the possibility of an afterlife, the fact that we can't prove that there is life after death isn't a valid reason to dismiss the idea; it's equally impossible to prove that there is **no** life after death. What has to be done in order to reach a reasonable conclusion about this (and indeed about anything) is to look at all the available evidence, theories and arguments, and then to make an informed judgment about what seems to be most probable.

But we can't do this all by ourselves. In all areas of life we have to rely on experts, authorities and specialists, who have studied the issues in much greater depth than we could hope to do. Even here we have to be cautious, for experts often disagree and no 'authority' should ever be accepted uncritically as having the last word on any subject, particularly on such a controversial one as a possible afterlife. Again we must think in terms of probable reliability, not infallibility, and ask what sort of qualifications and track record does the so-called expert have.

Relying provisionally in this way on experts and authorities is obviously the most reasonable and sensible approach in most areas of our everyday lives. Unless we have good reason for doing otherwise, we go to a doctor for medical help and a solicitor for legal advice, for example. Nowadays we also often use the Internet to get detailed technical information which previously we might have found in reference books, always remembering (if we're sensible) that none of these sources is infallible.

But who are the experts on life after death? Who on earth knows about an afterlife? What credentials or track record can we possibly look for here? Or, to put the question a slightly different way, which subjects or areas of knowledge may be most relevant and most likely to provide the best evidence? Let's start by looking at one obvious area, which has long been thought to offer the most authoritative evidence – religion.

Chapter 2

Can Religion Provide the Answers?

Traditionally, it has usually been thought that the place to look for answers is religion and that the experts on the afterlife are priests and theologians. We need to ask, then, whether religion should still be seen as the best (or even the only) source of reliable information on this subject. In what follows, the focus of our investigation will be mainly on Christianity, as that's the religion that probably most readers of this book (and its author) are most familiar with, and also because it illustrates particularly clearly how a religion can influence attitudes towards a possible afterlife. It goes without saying, however, that Christianity is only one of many religions, and other religions will be referred to where appropriate later in this book.

For centuries Christianity has offered a clear example of a religion exercising a monopoly (or some would say a stranglehold) over beliefs about life after death. This has conferred enormous power upon churches and priests, who have claimed to have privileged knowledge of what happens after death and of the requirements and rituals needed to ensure 'salvation' and avoid 'eternal damnation'. A notorious example of this exercise of power was the medieval sale of 'indulgences', offering so many days' remission from time needed to be spent in the intermediate state of purgatory before entry into heaven; even in the 20th century the Catholic Church was able to specify exactly how many days' remission could be granted by cardinals, bishops and archbishops. Today the Catholic Church still has a section on indulgences in its Catechism (1471), claiming that they can offer "remission from temporal punishment... through the action of the Church." An interesting modern example here is the offer of this remission to

Catholics who make the pilgrimage to the tomb of St. James in the Cathedral of Santiago, provided they collect the necessary stamps on the way and complete the last 100 kilometers on foot or horseback or the last 200 by bicycle. (I am grateful to Lesley Atkinson, who has followed the trail, for this information.)

The likelihood of death in battle has often increased the influence of religious authorities on beliefs about the afterlife. Before battles in medieval times, for example, soldiers would be 'shriven' by a priest to safeguard their souls if they were killed. More recently, in response to the slaughter of World War One, the Anglican Bishop of London (who will also feature in a later chapter) proclaimed: "Over every one who dies in this war with his face towards the foe, if he dies in Christ, will be said those words: 'This is My beloved son, in whom I am well pleased.'" Other clergy similarly assured their congregations that the man who died for England, no matter what kind of life he had previously led, would stand "cleansed from the stain of sin, crowned and triumphant, looking unto Jesus in the unveiled splendor of Paradise." (Kollar, 2000)

Such assurances would probably carry much less weight today. Religion, we are frequently told, is in a state of terminal decline, at least as far as Christianity in many Western countries is concerned. In the UK, for example, the numbers regularly attending most churches have been steadily dwindling for decades, as have the numbers of full-time clergy, who freely admit that they are struggling to 'keep the show on the road'. One in four parishes now have fewer than ten regular worshippers and overall numbers have halved since the 1960s. As a result, churches are being closed and it has been proposed that many may soon have to open only at Christmas and Easter. The Church features in the news mainly as an institution preoccupied with such issues such as women bishops, gay marriage and accusations of child abuse. Religious programs on radio and TV in the UK are banished to less popular time-slots. The media

11

tend to view religious believers as an eccentric and blinkered minority, while a formidable array of atheist intellectuals attack religion for the damage, division and bloodshed it has caused. What's more, they tell us, it is completely incompatible with the modern 'scientific world-view'. Religion portrays God as an 'Old Man in the Sky', whom we have to get on the right side of by prayer and worship to guarantee a place in an eternal Heaven and avoid an eternal Hell. This seems like childish nonsense, the argument goes, to all intelligent, rational people; we now live in a 'post-religious age'.

Similarly, in North America a recent study from San Diego State University of 58,000 interviewees suggested that the number of atheists has almost doubled since 1984, and that the number of Americans praying to and believing in God is at an all-time low. A significant increase was also evident in those having 'serious doubts' about the existence of God and those considering themselves 'not religious at all', particularly among younger people. By contrast, however, there had also been a slight increase in those who considered themselves 'spiritual', thus highlighting the problem of how to define belief in God or some higher power.

Yet while an obvious decline in orthodox religious belief and practice is evident in much of the Christian Church in Western countries, this doesn't necessarily tell us much about the overall standing or validity of 'religion' as such. A recent comprehensive survey of over 230 countries by the Pew Research Center found that more than 84% of the world population identified with or were affiliated to a religious group, though again much depends on definition here. Christianity, the largest religious grouping according to this survey with 32% of the world population, is not, of course, the only form that religion can take, and even within the Christian religion there is enormous variety and diversity.

Nevertheless, traditional Christian beliefs and concepts do

appear to have undeniably lost their appeal for many living in so-called 'secular' societies, who feel that they have outgrown their belief in Christianity and religion generally, just as they have given up believing in Father Christmas. Many children in the past, though, grew up with a much less benevolent idea of God than they had of Santa Claus. Karen Armstrong, theologian and former nun, in her monumental book, *A History of God* (1993), speaks of the liberating effect of getting rid of her childhood 'God': "It is wonderful not to have to cower before a vengeful deity, who threatens us with eternal damnation if we do not abide by his rules." The influential theologian and monk, Harry Williams, has written in a similar vein (1982) about how he suffered a nervous breakdown as a result of his view of God as an idol, whose back you had to scratch to keep him in a good mood.

The language in which the traditional creeds and doctrines of Christianity have been expressed, and are still expressed, doesn't resonate with (or even seem credible to) many who hold a modern world-view. Can we really believe that Man in the beginning 'fell' into a state of sin and could only be 'redeemed' from this by a God sacrificing his 'Son' in the form of Jesus, whom we must see as 'the Way, the Truth and the Life' if we are to be 'saved'? Can we accept that this Son, born of a virgin and attended by angels, "for our salvation came down and was made man, suffered, rose again on the third day, ascended into the heavens and will come to judge the living and the dead", as the Nicaean Creed states? Does the convoluted language used to define the 'Trinity', developed centuries after the birth of Christianity, make any sense today?

This decline in the traditional, orthodox beliefs and concepts of Christianity highlights the problems that can be caused when we try to define 'religion' in terms of specific doctrines and propositions which 'believers' have to give their assent to. These doctrines emerge from and become identified with a particular institutional 'religion'; 'being religious' thus comes to be understood as belonging to such an institution, accepting its doctrines and participating in its practices of worship and ritual. It follows that if you don't belong, accept and participate in this way, you're 'not religious', according to this definition.

This isn't the only way that religion can be defined, however. Much ink has been spilt over attempted definitions, and this isn't the place to add too much more to it. Some specialists have even denied that a satisfactory definition is possible; but the most general feature of religion that most would probably agree on is that it typically refers to the acceptance of a nonmaterial dimension, involving a belief in a divine or superhuman power (or 'God'). Even this raises big questions about the meaning of 'nonmaterial' and 'divine' and the many ways in which 'God' can be interpreted.

To avoid sinking further into this linguistic mire, we can find some illumination in an important distinction that was drawn over 100 years ago by the philosopher and psychologist, William James, in his classic study, *The Varieties of Religious Experience* (1960), a distinction between what he called institutional and personal religion. His bold approach in the book is to "ignore the institutional branch entirely, to say nothing of the ecclesiastical organization, to consider as little as possible the systematic theology and the ideas about the gods themselves, and to confine myself as far as I can to personal religion pure and simple." Whether or not "personal religion" can ever be called "pure and simple", James' distinction is a refreshing antidote to the popular image of religion, outlined above, which often assumes that a person's religion is wholly a matter of his or her attachment to an established religious institution. To place personal religious experience rather than membership of an institution at the heart of religion makes good sense when we realize that it was the personal visionary experiences of such figures as Jesus and Muhammad that preceded and finally resulted in the institutions which their followers created. We need to remember that Jesus was not a 'Christian', Buddha was not a 'Buddhist' and Muhammad was not a follower of Islam. All the major religious traditions and systems are the creations of those who followed and tried to institutionalize the original vision.

We shall return later to this distinction between personal and institutional religion and the importance of personal experience, but we first need to ask how the decline in traditional beliefs has affected attitudes towards a possible afterlife. Despite James' strategy of "ignoring the institutional branch entirely", the fact remains that most people today still assume that 'being religious' means belonging to a religious institution and subscribing to its doctrines. A related assumption is that believing in an afterlife depends on 'being religious' in this sense. The first example in our Introduction of a typical response to the question, "Do you believe in life after death?" was, "No, I'm not religious."

We might expect, then, that the decline in traditional Christian beliefs would be associated with a similar decline in afterlife beliefs. Surprisingly, however, the American research referred to above suggests that while orthodox religious beliefs and practices are on the wane, belief in an afterlife has increased, with almost 80% of those interviewed accepting the idea of life after death. This supports earlier research reported by the Institute of Education in London in 2012, which found that only 31% of those surveyed had a definite belief in God, while 49% believed that there was definitely or probably life after death.

These fascinating results suggest that the relationship between religious and afterlife beliefs is much more complex than we might suppose. Much will depend on which religious beliefs one accepts or rejects and what conception of an afterlife one holds. In particular, a rejection of some traditional afterlife beliefs may have contributed to the more general religious decline. The images of Heaven and Hell, for example, which have been prominent features of Christianity for most of its history, have fallen into disfavor. The theologian and former priest, Tom Harpur (1996), for example, has ridiculed the traditional view of heaven "with gates of gold and all that milk and honey... (and) endless choral efforts punctuated by the occasional sermon"; he also attributes the image of Hell as a fiery, eternal punishment to the Church's desire for control, noting that it has "caused an incalculable amount of suffering and harm here and now for millions of people." Harpur argues, as a Christian and Biblical scholar, that this concept of Hell does not represent the teaching of Jesus or of St. Paul.

The philosopher and theologian, John Hick (1985), similarly describes how the later account of Hell presented by Augustine in the fifth century "of bodies burning for ever and continuously suffering the intense pain of third-degree burns without either being consumed or losing consciousness is scientifically fantastic as it is morally revolting." It's difficult, in fact, to understand how anyone could reconcile the familiar Christian image of God as a loving father or a caring shepherd with one of a sadistic monster; loving fathers don't normally subject their erring children to endless torture, nor do caring shepherds inflict such treatment on straying sheep.

But surely no one accepts this view of Hell today, it might be objected. Many orthodox, conservative Christians would disagree. Richard Dawkins (2006), a fierce critic of religion, claims that in America today what may seem extreme to some is actually mainstream. He writes of his interview with a pastor in Colorado who offers parents and Christian schools the experience of Hell Houses for their children, showing them tableaux of 'sins' like homosexuality and abortion being punished by a scarlet-clothed Devil, "complete with realistic sulphurous smell of burning brimstone and the agonized screams of the forever damned."

While most people would claim to have grown out of

such literal conceptions of a Hell policed by gleeful demons and a Heaven filled with hymn-singing angels, it's easy to underestimate the unconscious influence that these images may continue to exert, particularly if they stem from childhood or adolescence. The testimony of Karen Armstrong and Father Harry Williams, quoted above, provide vivid examples of this influence and the effect it can have even upon experienced and sophisticated theologians.

Even though these ideas of Heaven and Hell are nowadays not widely accepted, however, the Christian Church is still assumed by many to be 'the authority' on matters concerning life after death. For centuries, millions have been buried according to the rites of the Church, and today many people see the inside of a church only when attending weddings or funerals. What they see and hear at traditional church funerals strengthens the impression that the afterlife is very much the province of religious professionals and certainly not the concern of those who see themselves as 'not religious'. Such people even appear to be excluded from any possible life after death by the words proclaimed at the start of most church funeral services: "I am the resurrection and the life, saith the Lord: he that believeth in me, though he were dead, yet shall he live: and whosoever liveth, and believeth in me shall never die." (*John, 11:25-6*) Hardly an encouraging message for one unable to believe in orthodox Christian doctrine.

But what does this doctrine actually say about life after death? The attender at a traditional church funeral will most probably hear these words of St. Paul delivered later in the service: "We shall not all sleep, but we shall all be changed, in a moment, in the twinkling of an eye, at the last trump: for the trumpet shall sound, and the dead shall be raised incorruptible, and we shall be changed." The service will also offer "sure and certain hope of the resurrection to eternal life through our Lord Jesus Christ who will transform our frail bodies that they may conform to his glorious body." (*Church of England Outline Order for Funerals*)

This offers a far from clear picture of what the believer (or nonbeliever) can expect at death. The traditional Christian view of the afterlife is in fact extremely difficult to elucidate, as it appears confused and contradictory to Christians and non-Christians alike. As the Rev. Allan Barham (1973), a minister who studied the issue of life after death in much more depth than most of his colleagues, argues, the general conception of heaven is not an altogether attractive one: "Some visualise it as a kind of unending church service, and even those with a love of music would hardly welcome such a prospect. Moreover, entry into heaven, it is sometimes taught, is to be preceded by 'the sleep of death', which may well last for an immense period of time. On the other hand, it is also taught that the moment after death we shall be in the full presence of Christ, for which most people would feel ill-prepared." He concludes that even among Christians there is often a feeling that the conventional idea of heaven is almost as unreal as the conventional idea of hell and that it is not surprising that public opinion polls show that very great numbers of those who call themselves Christians have no belief at all in a continuance of life in another state when they die.

Barham here puts his finger on some of the confusions that surround Christian doctrines of the afterlife. John Hick has documented these in his monumental work, *Death and Eternal Life*, referred to above, and we shall not investigate their historical and theological roots in further detail here. We don't need great theological expertise though to recognize that there is no one Christian doctrine of the afterlife. Do we at our death immediately find ourselves face to face with God (or Jesus), or do we fall into a comatose state to await 'judgment' at some future unspecified date, perhaps thousands or even millions years hence? These two possible scenarios are clearly incompatible with each other, so which is the official Christian 'party line'? The latter option (the 'Big Sleep'), which reflects St. Paul's teaching quoted above, seems for practical purposes to amount to little more than the nonbeliever's expectations of a state of unconscious nothingness following death, yet this is the implication of the message delivered at a traditional funeral service, reinforced by the frequent wording on gravestones – 'Rest in Peace'. The Catholic addition of the further afterlife states of Purgatory and Limbo has done nothing to lessen the confusion.

One doesn't have to be anti-religion or anti-Christian to endorse the above criticisms. As Barham says, it's not surprising that great numbers of those who call themselves Christian have no belief in life after death. Even those who profess to have such a belief are often reluctant to reflect in any depth on the subject and appear embarrassed to talk about it. This is splendidly (and humorously) illustrated in an anecdote related by Frederic Myers, the scholar and researcher whom we have already met in Chapter 1. Myers was fascinated by the whole question of survival of death and an afterlife. Finding himself one day seated at dinner next to a distinguished businessman of firm Christian beliefs, he steered the conversation towards his favorite issue. The man became rather uncomfortable and tried to change the subject, but Myers persisted and finally asked directly what the man's idea of life after death really was. There was an awkward pause before he replied, "Well I suppose we shall enter into the joy of the Lord. But why bring up such an unpleasant subject?"

If even professed Christians have found Christian doctrines contradictory and the whole question of life after death embarrassing and "unpleasant", it's perhaps surprising that the Church maintained its position as the unquestioned authority on the subject for so long. Probably this was because there were no real contenders to challenge that authority. This was about to change, however, when there appeared on the scene during the

19th century two strong challengers whose influence is still felt in various ways – spiritualism and psychical research. We shall see in the following chapters how the Church reacted to these threats and how the resulting conflict throws much light on our own search today for information about a possible afterlife.

Chapter 3

The Challenge of Spiritualism

The first threat came from a most unlikely source – two young girls living in a small house in the little hamlet of Hydesville in New York State. Kate and Margaretta Fox had become so alarmed by repeated mysterious knockings and other noises in their home that they refused to sleep apart and were taken into their parents' room. The knockings continued and increased, however, until on the night of March 31st 1848, the 11-year-old Kate Fox issued a challenge to whatever was causing the disturbances. Her mother in a statement given four days later described what happened when her youngest child, Kate, said, "'Mr. Splitfoot, do as I do,' clapping her hands. The sound instantly followed her with the same number of raps. When she stopped, the sound ceased for a short time. Then Margaretta said, 'Now, do just as I do. Count one, two, three, four,' striking one hand against the other at the same time. The raps came as before and she was afraid to repeat them."

Mrs. Fox then took up the questioning and was told the correct ages of her children. Using the raps to establish a simple form of code, she was told that they were coming from an "injured spirit", a man of 31, who had been murdered in the house and buried in the cellar. Neighbors flocked to the house on hearing of this and, in the absence of Mrs. Fox and her daughters, elicited further responses from the continuing raps. Soon after, human hair and bone were found in the cellar, but it was not until 1904 that further excavations brought to light an almost entire human skeleton between the earth and the crumbling cellar walls.

The origins of modern spiritualism are usually traced back to these events in Hydesville, which were exhaustively investigated and became the subject of huge controversy amid claims and counterclaims of trickery. The details of these and of the subsequent checkered history of the Fox family have been fully documented by many writers and need not concern us here. The Hydesville incident is highly relevant to our inquiry, however, for two reasons.

Firstly, it marked the beginning of the rapid spread and development of spiritualism. The movement grew with dramatic speed in North America among all classes of society to such an extent that an early investigator, Judge John W. Edmonds, could write only four years after Hydesville that there were ten or twelve newspapers and periodicals devoted to the cause and that the "spiritual library" already embraced more than 100 different publications, some of which had attained a circulation of more than 10,000 copies. Readers included doctors, lawyers and clergymen in great numbers, a Protestant bishop, the president of a college, judges, members of Congress, foreign ambassadors and ex-members of the United States Senate (Doyle, 1926).

Spiritualism's speedy growth was not limited to North America. It soon reached Great Britain and extended into mainland Europe. Again the details of this general development have been fully described by other researchers and are not the subject of the present book, though the impact that spiritualism made in the UK during and after the First World War will be examined in later chapters, as these events focus the spotlight particularly sharply upon the conflict with the Christian church.

The second reason why Hydesville and the spread of spiritualism are relevant to our inquiry is directly related to that potential conflict. As described in the previous chapter, the Christian church had for centuries been seen in the West (and saw itself) as the authority on all matters relating to life after death and as the necessary intermediary between the people and God in such matters. Now, for the first time, that exclusive role of intermediary was being challenged by the public awareness of an alternative – the medium. A medium didn't need to have any religious position or credentials, nor even to belong to any church, in order to offer apparent access to those who had died. It's easy to understand the strong appeal of spiritualism and the popularity of mediums, despite the many accusations of fraud that were soon being made. Spiritualism was not exclusive, not tied to religious professionals and not dependent on theological jargon. It also offered recognition and status to the many women mediums, in contrast to the male domination of positions held in the established Church.

It would be a huge mistake, however, to assume that an apparent ability to contact 'spirits' first appeared in North America in the 19th century. Interaction with the spirit world, particularly with dead ancestors, including various forms of spirit 'possession', had for millennia been a feature of many ancient cultures and religions. Mediums in ancient China, for example, practiced forms of automatic writing, not unlike those developed in modern spiritualism. A century before the Hydesville event, the Swedish seer and mystic, Emanuel Swedenborg, displayed many apparent psychical powers, including communication with spirits and visits to the afterlife; as a result, some have regarded him as the father of modern spiritualism.

The post-Hydesville mediums, however, though resembling their predecessors in some ways, offered a distinctively personal and direct attraction for the general public. Some mediums may have gone into trance to obtain communications, but they were not 'possessed' by the spirits of ancestors. Typically, mediums would (and still do) attempt to relay information from specific individuals who had died, often family members or close friends, who would at times provide factual information intended to prove their identity. This type of communication could be enormously comforting to the recipient, apparently demonstrating that death was not the end and that their loved ones were still fully conscious and eager to make contact.

The understandable popularity of spiritualism, then, posed a serious threat to the authority of the Christian Church. The American writer, Oliver Wendell Holmes, described this threat as "the Nemesis of the pulpit". Writing in 1860, twelve years after Hydesville, he eloquently declared that spiritualism was quietly undermining the traditional ideas of the afterlife "ending with such a crack of old beliefs that the roar of it is heard in all the ministers' studies of Christendom!" (Holmes, 1860)

Ministers and theologians were not slow to respond to this 'plague'. One favorite method of defence was to accuse spiritualism of being 'unbiblical', invoking 'devilish spirits' and indulging in the forbidden practice of 'necromancy', a charge vigorously rejected by spiritualists. (We shall see later how this emotive term continued to arouse passions on both sides well into the 20th century.)

These Christian attacks on spiritualism originated in America, where it was estimated that séances were attracting hundreds of thousands of interested members of the public. The rapid spread of the movement to Europe, however, was accompanied by equally fierce denunciations from all branches of the Church. Catholic opposition was particularly vehement. In Italy, for example, the widely read Jesuit journal, *Civiltá Cattolica*, in 1853 declared spiritualism to be "a work of the Devil, a tangle of blasphemies, of contradictions, of brazen absurdities; frauds accepted by a faithless and credulous people." A Sicilian priest was excommunicated, driven out of his parish, brought to trial and imprisoned for supporting spiritualism. The Bishop of Barcelona burned 300 copies of spiritualist books in the city square in 1861 (Biondi, 2013).

These examples of the bitter conflict between spiritualism and the Christian Church following the events at Hydesville could be elaborated at length, but enough has been said to show how disturbed the Church authorities were by this new development. The response in the UK was probably more restrained than in many other countries and will not be examined at this point. The confrontation here came to a head at a later date in a way that further highlighted the root causes of the clash, as we shall see in upcoming chapters.

Before this was to take place, however, the ground in the UK was being prepared for the challenge of the medium to the minister by a much less dramatic event than the Hydesville saga. This originated in a very different setting and attracted far less public attention, but it was to have an equally powerful influence on attempts to explore a possible afterlife.

Chapter 4

The Challenge of Psychical Research

The courtyard of a Cambridge University College seems far removed from a modest cottage in suburban America, but it's not too far-fetched to locate the origins of the main British contribution to the afterlife controversy in that serene environment. This was where a conversation took place one night in December 1871, 23 years after the Hydesville incident, between two academics gazing at the stars. They were Frederic Myers, whom we've already met in this book, and Henry Sidgwick. Both men were classical scholars and much more besides. Myers' areas of expertise extended into the areas of philosophy, psychology, science, history and poetry. Sidgwick likewise was an eminent moral philosopher, with a deep interest in the relationship between religion and science. Both men also shared a much more unusual passion – the investigation of 'spirit communication'.

Sidgwick had been encouraged to explore this subject by his cousin, Edward Benson, hardly a nonentity himself, as he would later become Archbishop of Canterbury. Benson had helped to form a 'Ghost Society' at Cambridge, which enabled Sidgwick to investigate some local mediums (who failed to impress him). Myers was equally fascinated by the possibility of rigorous research into life after death, which might be a means of bridging what seemed to be an ever-widening gulf between religion and modern scientific ideas.

On that starry night in 1871 Myers later described how he had asked Sidgwick whether he thought that a study of ghosts and spirits could reveal something of what might lie beyond the physical, material, mortal world. Sidgwick replied that such a study might well offer insights into unexplored worlds; but who would be prepared to undertake this kind of research?

Fortunately, Myers and Sidgwick were not lone voices in wishing to probe these subjects in the UK. The naturalist, Alfred Russel Wallace, coauthor of Charles Darwin's theory of natural selection, was another enthusiast, as were the physicist, William Barrett, and the eminent chemist and inventor, William Crookes, who was already investigating the remarkable effects produced by the medium, D.D. Home. Another prominent pioneer researcher was Edmund Gurney, a Cambridge student of law and philosophy.

These men, eleven years after Myers' and Sidgwick's moonlit conversation, helped to found the British Society for Psychical Research, which held its first meeting in February 1882, and is still going strong today over 130 years later. The early membership quickly grew to over 200, including many well-known figures such as Alfred, Lord Tennyson, John Ruskin, Charles Dodgson (*aka* Lewis Carroll) and Arthur Balfour, later to become Prime Minister.

The Society also soon attracted the attention and support of the American psychologist and philosopher, William James, quoted in the previous chapter, who helped to found the American Society for Psychical Research just three years after its British counterpart. "The evidence published by the English society," commented the first circular of the American Society, "is of a nature not to be ignored by scientific men."

That statement highlighted some of the significant differences in approach between the pioneers of psychical research and the spiritualist movement which had sprung from Hydesville. The aim of the Society for Psychical Research (from now on to be referred to as the SPR) was and still is stated to be "to examine without prejudice or prepossession and in a scientific spirit those faculties of man, real or supposed, which appear to be inexplicable on any generally recognized hypothesis." William James, on behalf of the American Society (from now on to be referred to as the ASPR), similarly declared, "What we want is not only truth, but evidence." From the start, then, both societies aspired to be **scientific** bodies, adhering to **scientific** principles and procedures. Half of the SPR Presidents since its foundation have been university professors of science or philosophy. One of its early Presidents, who will play a leading part in later chapters, Sir Oliver Lodge, wrote (1909) that the Society was intended to nurture "a spirit of genuine 'scepticism' – that is to say, of critical examination and inquiry, not of dogmatic denial and assertion. No phenomenon was to be unhesitatingly rejected because at first sight incredible. No phenomenon was to be accepted which could not make its position good by crucial and convincing tests."

This aim of scientific rigor did not prevent the SPR and the ASPR from soon becoming as much a target of controversy and criticism as was spiritualism, though for rather different reasons. As academic bodies they attracted the hostility of many academics who felt that such activities were not 'real science'. The subject of psychical research or parapsychology is still dismissed in this way by many today, despite the fact that parapsychologists can now be found in a number of university psychology departments, doing controlled experimental research work. Many scientists are antagonistic to the whole subject, displaying varying degrees of skepticism and dogmatic rejection, often to the point of refusing even to look at the evidence available.

On the other hand, the SPR also faced opposition from an entirely different direction, as it was accused by spiritualists and others convinced of the reality of psychical phenomena (including mediumistic communications) of being too cautious in not openly validating such phenomena. One source of criticism that the SPR did share with the spiritualists stemmed from some religious quarters. Henry Sidgwick in a Presidential Address to the Society commented: "There are not a few religious persons who see no reason to doubt our alleged facts, but who regard any experimental investigation of them as wrong, because they must be the work either of the Devil or of familiar spirits, with whom the Bible forbids us to have dealings. Their scruples have really no place in the present stage of our investigation."

This was not the only common feature shared by psychical research and spiritualism. Despite their obvious differences in approach and ethos, both placed great importance upon mediums and their apparent ability to receive communications from the dead. Mediumship was, of course, crucial in the birth of spiritualism, as we've seen. The movement soon developed in different directions, resulting in a wide array of groups and organizations, all calling themselves spiritualist, though often disagreeing on religious or philosophical grounds. Yet what all spiritualist organizations have always had in common is a belief that mediumship is a major route by which the spirits of the dead can hold communication with the living.

The SPR and the ASPR were never spiritualist organizations. Most of their members would not have counted themselves as spiritualists, and conversely few spiritualists would have described themselves as psychical researchers. From its outset, the SPR has investigated a very wide range of phenomena, which include (but are by no means limited to) hauntings and apparitions, telepathy and extrasensory perception, premonitions, psychokinesis (the movement of objects by nonphysical means), out-of-the-body experiences, near-death experiences and reincarnation. Nevertheless, it's fair to say that studies of mediumship have played a major role in its activities throughout its history.

Mediumship provided plenty of scope for the pioneers of psychical research, as the rapid growth of spiritualism had encouraged an equally rapid growth in fraud and deception on the part of some mediums. One early SPR researcher, Richard

Hodgson, commented in a report of 1886: "I may conclude with a warning, which I wish to give especially to our members in America, viz: that nearly all professional mediums are a gang of vulgar tricksters who are more or less in league with one another." The ASPR was already regularly exposing fraudulent mediums, leading one of their researchers to judge that they were "at worst liars and cheats, at best victims of a mental illness that caused self-delusion," charges that have been regularly repeated ever since (Blum, 2007).

Much of the early psychical research into mediumship, then, focused on discrediting mediums who were found to be fraudulent. This approach, however, was thought to be too negative by some, including William James, who was himself investigating a medium whom his mother-in-law had introduced to him, Mrs. Leonora Piper, who was destined to become one of the most famous figures in the history of psychical research. James had already had plenty of experience of fake mediums before he first met Mrs. Piper, but he soon decided that Mrs. Piper was in a completely different category. At his first anonymous sitting she provided accurate information about his family members, including the name of his baby son, who had recently died. Mrs. Piper continued to impress James and other researchers, and in 1889 was persuaded, much against her will, to travel to England to be assessed by members of the SPR. For many years thereafter she continued to supply psychical researchers on both sides of the Atlantic with some of the strongest evidence for life after death ever provided. William James' final verdict was that he would be willing to stake as much money on Mrs. Piper's honesty as on that of anyone he knew, while James Hyslop, a leading SPR investigator, despite his initial skepticism, eventually declared that she had been subjected to the most stringent tests for decades without once being found wanting.

The details of her long and remarkable career have been

well-documented and would fill many books, but that isn't the purpose of this one. Mrs. Piper's importance for our present purposes was twofold. First, she provided the pioneer psychical researchers with compelling evidence that not all mediums could be dismissed as money-grabbing charlatans. Secondly, one of the British researchers she cooperated with was a figure whom we have already met briefly and who will play a major role in the following chapters, Sir Oliver Lodge. He concluded that no conceivable deception on her part could explain the facts he had personally witnessed.

It seems, then, a strange coincidence that this period in the mid-nineteenth century should have seen the birth of two movements, spiritualism and psychical research, which despite their obvious differences and antagonism both presented a formidable challenge to the status of orthodox religion as the authority on all matters concerning life after death. This was because both highlighted the phenomenon of mediumship and the possibility of communication with those who had died. We saw in the previous chapter how religious figures initially responded to this challenge. In the UK, however, the conflict came to a head somewhat later, as a result of a much more bloody conflict, the First World War. Events during and after that War throw further light on the clash between medium and minister. A detailed exploration of this clash will help to clarify the main issues surrounding the question which still faces us today – how can we know anything about a possible afterlife?

Chapter 5

Messages from the Front

On September 14th, 1915 a young British officer was killed in the front line at Ypres. He was hit by a shell while helping to dig a trench and died shortly afterwards. The standard telegram to his family from the King and Queen read, "The King and Queen deeply regret the loss you and the army have sustained by the death of your son in the service of his country. Their Majesties truly sympathize with you in your sorrow." Such telegrams were frequently sent at that time, for this officer was just one of a multitude of soldiers to die in the conflict. There was nothing remarkable about this death, then, in the overall context of the War, and on the face of it nothing especially significant. It could be argued, however, that this single death had more momentous consequences than any other of the millions that occurred during the War; for the officer's name was Raymond Lodge and he was the son of Sir Oliver Lodge.

We saw in the last chapter how Lodge had played an important part in the development of psychical research in the UK and in the early activities of the SPR.

His investigation of the American medium, Mrs. Piper, had convinced him of the survival of personality and the possibility of communication with the dead, but Lodge was far from being a starry-eyed spiritualist and was never a member of any spiritualist organization. He was in fact one of the most eminent scientists of his day, having been knighted for his pioneering work on electricity, magnetism, radiation and telegraphy. This did not prevent him, however, from pursuing his studies of mediumship, in the role of a cautious, tough-minded researcher.

A month before Raymond Lodge's death a message was communicated to his father through Mrs. Piper in America, claiming to be from Frederic Myers who had died in 1901. This seemed to warn Lodge that a heavy blow was about to fall on him which Myers, a former friend and colleague, would help to alleviate. The warning was given by a reference to a poem by the Roman poet, Horace. (Myers had apparently lost none of his classical knowledge!) Soon after Raymond's death, Lodge and his wife had anonymous sittings with another medium in London, Mrs. Gladys Leonard, which appeared to confirm this message and to come from Raymond himself. The communicator told Lodge that 'M.' was helping him and that he felt he "had two fathers now... my old one and another too." This was the start of a long series of sittings that Lodge and various members of his family were to have with a number of different mediums. The remarkably specific information communicated during these convinced them all that Raymond Lodge was indeed in contact with them on a regular basis.

A year after Raymond's death his father published the first edition of a book about his son and the many apparent communications the family had received from him – that book, entitled *Raymond, or Life and Death* (1916), would soon become a classic text in the history of psychical research. It quickly became very popular as we can see from the fact that it ran into six editions in just over a month (something most authors only dream about) and had reached ten editions by the end of the War. It also became popular in America, Australia and on the Continent. The book is still in print today over 100 years later and attracting excellent reviews from modern readers.

What made the book so outstanding was the sheer weight of evidence for Raymond's survival that his father presents and the very rigorous and cautious approach that he adopts in distinguishing between what he calls evidential and non-evidential material. Many different sitters and mediums were involved and a lot of information was given which was completely unknown to the sitters. For example, there was the famous incident of the photograph of Raymond taken shortly before his death, showing him with a group of officers, which he describes in precise detail **long before** his family even knew that such a photograph existed. On another occasion Oliver Lodge sets up a test during a sitting when he asks if Raymond remembers Mr. Jackson. Raymond replies through the medium, "He fell down. Put him on a pedestal." Mr. Jackson was in fact a peacock, resident in the Lodge's garden who had just died and who was about to be stuffed and put on a pedestal, a fact completely unknown to the medium.

The book contained many examples of this kind, illustrating what seemed to be the joint efforts of the living father and the dead son to produce the best possible evidence they could for life after death and the survival of the individual personality. Oliver Lodge was meticulous in his analysis and assessment of the evidence produced in the many sittings he and his family had with various mediums, and as President of the SPR he had access to the best mediums available at that time. Raymond for his part seemed to enjoy cooperating fully with his father's investigations and going out of his way to provide watertight evidence of his identity.

Raymond didn't just try to provide his father with evidence of survival, however. He also had a lot to say about the conditions and the environment he was experiencing, and the work he was doing with other soldiers killed in action. He speaks about the different levels or spheres of the afterlife, and how one gravitates to the level one is best suited to as a result of one's spiritual development or lack of it. Oliver Lodge, as cautious as ever, left out some of these descriptions from the book, as they were not in his words "evidential matter". This challenging problem of how to assess alleged accounts of afterlife conditions will be discussed later in this book.

However, some of the material that was included in the book was seized on by critics eager to discredit everything in it and to reject all the evidence for life after death that it offered. One passage in particular attracted ridicule, where Raymond claimed that in the transition period after death it was possible to create the counterparts of physical objects found on earth such as cigars. He described how "a chap came over the other day who would have a cigar," but that "when he began to smoke it, he didn't think so much of it and now he doesn't look at one." Later writers have pointed out that such reports are not necessarily as laughable as they may appear, as other communications paint a similar picture of the early stages of the afterlife where apparently 'physical' objects can be reproduced, perhaps to ease the abrupt transition involved in leaving the physical world. We shall look at these reports in more detail in Chapter 17 at the end of our investigation.

The impact of Lodge's book was enormous and so was the amount of controversy it caused, as we shall shortly see. But Lodge was not alone in publicizing the psychical evidence for survival of death during the War. Another even more well-known public figure, who had also been knighted for services to his country, was treading a similar path.

Chapter 6

The Man Who Created Sherlock Holmes

If popular 'celebrities' had been as prominent in the media a hundred years ago as they are today, one man would certainly have been in great demand. Sir Arthur Conan Doyle was a famous name, largely because of the fascination the public had (and continues to have) with his immortal creation, Sherlock Holmes, perhaps the best-known and most enduring literary figure of all time. Conan Doyle's attempt to 'kill off' the detective at the hands of Professor Moriarty in 1893 because he was tired of him had been met with universal shock and protest, and he had reluctantly had to relent ten years later by bringing Holmes back from the dead.

The Holmes stories, then, had made Conan Doyle a household name, but that was far from being his only claim to fame. As an author, his output covered many areas in addition to his detective stories. He wrote historical novels (which he considered his best work), science fiction, military histories, light domestic novels, verse, plays and a vast variety of short stories on all sorts of themes. His literary work, however, was only one facet of a life of astonishing variety and achievement, packed with adventure and drama, which kept him constantly in the public eye. Born in 1859 in Edinburgh into a large Catholic family, he was educated at Catholic boarding schools, which turned him against religious dogma for life. He qualified as a doctor at Edinburgh University and practiced for a number of years, doing his writing as a sideline, until the success of the first Sherlock Holmes short stories persuaded him that he might be able to earn his living as an author. He was also an outstanding sportsman, excelling at cricket, football, boxing and billiards, to name but a few of his athletic pastimes, and reaching near-professional standard at some of these. He was a pioneer motorist and rally-driver, and introduced ski-touring to Switzerland in the 1890s.

Apart from his sporting prowess, he stood twice for Parliament and narrowly missed being elected. He worked as a war correspondent in Egypt and helped to run a field hospital in South Africa during the Boer War. He conducted long and successful campaigns on behalf of two men whom he believed had been wrongly convicted of serious crimes. He was a leading figure in advocating military, naval and divorce reform, and was always ready to voice his opinions on current issues in the Press.

Among his many interests and enthusiasms there was one which the general public was probably less aware of. He had had a long-standing involvement in the study of psychical research in general and the possibility of surviving physical death in particular, attending his first spiritualist lecture on "Does Death End All?" in Birmingham in 1880. While practicing as a young doctor in Southsea in the 1880s, his interest was further stimulated by his active membership of the Portsmouth Literary and Scientific Society, and as a result he experimented with telepathy and table-tilting. In 1887 he took part in a number of sittings with a medium and sent a letter to the journal *Light* describing his experiences. He joined the SPR in 1893 and under its auspices in the following year investigated a case of apparent poltergeist activity. In 1894 he attended a lecture by Frederic Myers on "Recent Evidences as to Man's Survival after Death". His deep interest in psychical issues was at times reflected in his literary work. One of his earliest short stories, *The Captain of the Polestar*, published in 1883 and judged by some to be one of the finest ghost stories in the English language, describes an apparition which haunts the captain of a ship in Arctic waters; it also features a brief discussion of spiritualism.

For many years, however, he maintained a cautious attitude

towards psychical issues, particularly those regarding life after death. "The subject of psychical research," he wrote in 1918, "is one upon which I have thought more, and about which I have been slower to form my opinion, than upon any other subject whatever." Unlike Oliver Lodge, he was not convinced about our survival of physical death. In 1915 in the midst of the huge loss of life in the War, when asked by the *International Psychic Gazette*, "What would you say in consolation to those in grief? How would you help?" his brief response was, "I fear I can say nothing worth saying. Time only is the healer." (Carr, 1949)

Yet just a year later in 1916, the year of Raymond Lodge's death, Conan Doyle publicly declared his broad acceptance of the spiritualist philosophy, "where faith is replaced by actual demonstration." In 1917 he gave his first public lecture on the subject entitled "The New Revelation" at the London Spiritualists Alliance, and he took the same title for his first spiritualist book, published in 1918.

So what finally compelled Conan Doyle in that momentous year of 1916 to throw his weight unequivocally behind the spiritualist position? The turning-point for him was a particular personal experience, which he saw as providing conclusive evidence for our survival of death. "I know no single argument," he wrote, "which is not in favour of the extinction of our individuality at death, save only the facts of psychical research, but these are so strong that they must outweigh all others." The clinching argument for Conan Doyle involved information transmitted to him apparently from his brother-in-law, who had been killed in 1914. The communication was obtained through the automatic writing of a family friend and referred to a private conversation between the two men, which only Conan Doyle himself was now aware of.

By 1916, then, both Lodge and Conan Doyle had had personal experiences of psychical communication which convinced them that death was not the end. Conan Doyle had to wait until late

1918 and early 1919, however, for his convictions to be fully tested and that was in the most shattering way. In quick succession he lost his son, Kingsley, and his only brother, Innes, to the great influenza pandemic. Both of them had fought in the War and been weakened as a result. Like Oliver Lodge, Conan Doyle would soon have his acceptance of personal survival further strengthened by what he believed to be direct communication from his son, brother and other family members. "There is never a month, often never a week, that I do not commune with him," he later wrote.

By the end of the War, then, both men were convinced of the fact of survival as a result of their personal experiences with mediums and their assessment of the evidence. Both men had by then also made momentous decisions. If these things were true that had been clearly demonstrated to them, they had a duty, an obligation, to do all they could to publicize these truths to as wide an audience as possible – in other words, they had a mission and, as we shall see, it was to be a mission that they would both pursue for the rest of their lives. That mission was destined to put the two men on a collision course with the Church, as it would challenge its claim to be the ultimate authority on life after death. The conflict between medium and minister in the UK was about to intensify and to throw into sharp relief that question at the heart of this book – who on earth knows about the afterlife?

Chapter 7

Two Knights on a Mission

The two knights whom we have just met, Sir Oliver Lodge and Sir Arthur Conan Doyle, found fertile ground in 1916 for their mission to publicize the evidence that death was not the end. Lodge wrote of the "appalling amount of premature and unnatural bereavement" that the War was creating. "The pain caused by exposing one's own sorrow and its alleviation to possible scoffers, becomes almost negligible," he revealed in *Raymond*, "in view of the service which it is legitimate to hope may thus be rendered to mourners, if they can derive comfort by learning that communication across the gulf is possible."

Conan Doyle felt that his mission was driven by the same impetus. "In the presence of an agonized world," he wrote (1918), rather more eloquently than Lodge, "hearing every day of the deaths of the flower of our race in the first promise of their unfulfilled youth, seeing around one the wives and mothers who had no clear conception whither their lived one had gone, I seemed suddenly to see that this subject with which I had so long dallied was not merely a study of a force outside the rules of science, but that it was really something tremendous, a breaking down of the walls between two worlds, a direct undeniable message from beyond, a call of hope and of guidance to the human race at the time of its deepest affliction."

The two knights had caught the mood of the time perfectly. Both men began to receive huge post bags from the bereaved, thanking them for the support they had gained from their message of hope. Why was that support so welcome at this time? Largely because it was becoming increasingly clear that for many people the Church, which one might have expected to be the obvious source of spiritual help in such a crisis, was failing to meet the psychological and spiritual needs of many of the bereaved. What did the Church seem to be offering? The Bishop of London, for example, admitted in 1918, that "we have not sufficiently preached the Gospel of Hope to the mourners" and that "we must go back to a much brighter view of death than we now have in the Church." The Archbishop of Canterbury emphasized the need for faith and spoke of "the shadow of bereavement. ... and the sigh of a bewildered and wondering heart."

Conan Doyle blamed the Church for "cold comfort administered to those who mourn their dead" and for "windy words and dogmatic assertions prevailing in the pulpit." Criticism was even coming from within the Church. A committee of military chaplains spoke of "the crying need of a simple form of devotion" and called for more adequate provision to satisfy the widespread desire for Prayers for the Dead (Kollar, 2000).

What form did the two knights' mission take to counter the "cold comfort" of the Church? Conan Doyle dedicated the last fourteen years of his life to presenting as forcefully as he could to as wide an audience as possible the evidence for our survival of physical death (Straughan, 2013). During this period he lectured in practically every major town and city in the UK – but that wasn't nearly enough for him. He felt he had to take his message to every corner of the globe, and so undertook lengthy lecture tours to Australia, New Zealand, North America, South Africa and Scandinavia, taking his whole family with him. He attracted enormous audiences and enormous controversy. Wherever he went he had sittings with mediums, assessed their quality and wrote about his findings. He took part in high profile public debates on the subject. He wrote extensively about it, including a comprehensive history of spiritualism, which he dedicated to Oliver Lodge. One of his last acts, when critically ill with heart disease, was to travel to London in 1930 to petition the Home Secretary for a change in the law concerning the prosecution of mediums. That effort finally killed him.

Oliver Lodge didn't cover so many miles as Conan Doyle, but he gave numerous lectures and newspaper interviews and took part in many debates about the psychical evidence for life after death. "Thousands flock to hear Sir Oliver Lodge," said one press cutting, "Amazing scenes at a church in Glasgow. 7-800 were unable to get in, traffic was held up and Sir Oliver was called upon to give his sermon twice." As a leading scientist, he even used his presidency of the British Association to publicize the issue. Like Conan Doyle he attracted a lot of criticism. He spoke of the "ridicule and dislike" poured upon his beliefs. He was accused of "necromancy, witchcraft and dealings with the unseen." His book, *Raymond*, was attacked by one critic as "nauseating drivel" that "sullies the fair name of science."

The two men were also a joint target of the Bishop of London, mentioned above, who claimed that it was a sin to seek to know what we could not know: "Let Sir Oliver Lodge and Sir Conan Doyle [he couldn't even get the name right!] do what they like," he declared, "but do not let the ordinary mourner spend his hours trying to get into communication with the dead." Further virulent criticism of the two men came from the direction of the Catholic Church. Father Bernard Vaughan, a Jesuit priest, saw the Devil's hand in their work. "I would rather be in prison for the rest of my life," he thundered, "than carry on the work that is being done by these two gentlemen," whom he accused of "having lost their mental poise," by indulging in necromancy and "gulping down van loads of rubbish which ought to be tilted on a rubbish heap." (Wingett, 2016)

Most of the hostility directed towards the two knights both before and after the War came from traditional, orthodox elements within the Churches. One speaker at the 1919 Church Congress at Leicester, for example, challenged Conan Doyle "to deny, if he dare, that this thing involves a great peril to the mental, moral and spiritual life." Another speaker declared,

"Necromancy, that is, dealing with the dead, is forbidden in the Scriptures. It is wrong." (Kollar, 2000) Necromancy was obviously the buzz word at that Church Congress. Dean Inge spoke of "poor souls going back to the old discredited, barbarous superstitions of necromancy.... Astrology, witchcraft and other mischievous delusions have once more stalked out into the light of day," he asserted.

Conan Doyle, of course, was having none of this. In the same week as that Church Congress he spoke to a full house at the Palace Theatre in Leicester and went on to address the attack. He declared:

> **"Dean Inge may ill-treat us, but he must not ill-treat the King's English. He charges us with necromancy. This is derived from the Greek word 'nekron', (a corpse) and the word really means incantations round a corpse. But we look upon a corpse as matter; we have nothing to do with it. We deal with the spiritual body as St Paul taught. The corpse is gone. So if he had hunted through the dictionary from end to end he could not have got a worse word to describe our belief. We have no room for Dismal Deans. If we could get him with us we would soon stop him being dismal." (Laughter from audience!)**
> **(Doyle, 1920)**

It would be a mistake, however, to assume in view of all this opposition from religious quarters that the two knights were anti-religious. So what precisely were their religious beliefs and how did they integrate them with their psychical experiences and convictions?

Both men were sympathetic towards spiritualism, but neither saw it as an independent religion in its own right. On the contrary, they went out of their way to emphasize, as Conan Doyle put it, that spiritualism was a system of thought and knowledge which could be reconciled with any religion. "I trust," he wrote, "that it will not crystallise into a new religion. I see it as the great unifying force, the one provable thing connected with every religion, Christian or non-Christian." (Doyle, 1938) Spiritualism for him didn't depend on faith and acceptance of doctrines that were unprovable and to many unbelievable. It offered knowledge, evidence and facts, backed by personal experience.

Even so, the religious foundation for both men was firmly Christian. Oliver Lodge was the more orthodox of the two and he frequently wrote and spoke about his Christian faith. "I think of Christ," he declared in one interview, "as the highest manifestation of Deity able to show itself in human form… He came and lived and died to unify man with God. That is the meaning of his Saviourhood and His AT-ONE-MENT." Lodge's Christian beliefs didn't stop him, however, from attacking the Church's attitude to spiritualism: "The spirit of the inquisition is not yet dead," he wrote after that 1919 Church Congress. "If communication is feasible, no Church has a right to forbid it." In his view, "There is nothing in the Spiritualistic creed… which is alien to the Christian faith." (Kollar, 2000) What needed to be changed were "the doctrines men have invented and foisted on the pure Gospel of Christ."

Conan Doyle was even more radical and critical of those traditional church doctrines. He argued that "far too much stress has been laid upon Christ's death, and far too little upon his life, where the true grandeur lay." As a result, the human race had "lost itself in vain dreams of vicarious sacrifice and imaginary falls, with all the mystical and contentious philosophy which has centred round the subject." Christianity, he declared, must change or perish. He also argued for a psychical interpretation of the New Testament, arguing that the early Christian Church was "saturated with spiritualism", and giving many Biblical examples of psychical events and powers.

As with Oliver Lodge, then, spiritualism for Conan Doyle was entirely compatible with Christianity. He even campaigned for a specifically Christian principle to be incorporated in the set of basic spiritualist beliefs, claiming that a European spiritualist should in a broad sense be a Christian. "How strange," he commented, "that the Church should attack us for confirming its own doctrine of immortality, its basic creed." Both the Church and spiritualism, he maintained, had a common enemy in materialism, and they should combine to fight it. He challenged the Church leaders on this point: "Come in and help us fight the materialism of the world. We are (your) strongest allies... yet all you can do is turn upon us and try to rend us." (Doyle, 1920) This offer (not surprisingly) seemed to fall on deaf ears. On another occasion he remarked, "Wherever I go, there are two great types of critics. One is the materialistic gentleman who insists on his right to eternal nothingness. The other is the gentleman with such a deep respect for the Bible that he has never looked into it." (Carr, 1949)

There was an even more direct link, however, between the two men's mission and their religious convictions. Both believed that that mission was divinely inspired and guided. "If I can be used by Higher Powers to bear testimony to truth," wrote Lodge at the end of his autobiography, "then, whether palatable or not, that is all I ask. Whatever happens to me, I rejoice in the opportunity of service, and am thankful for the kindly help and guidance always forthcoming." Conan Doyle expressed very similar sentiments in his autobiography: "In the days of universal sorrow and loss... it was borne in upon me that the knowledge which had come to me was not for my own consolation alone, but that God had placed me in a very special position for conveying it to that world which needed it so badly."

The two knights, then, believed that their mission was divinely directed. That strengthened them to act as prophets of hope and to spare no effort in spreading their message to thousands, perhaps millions, of people who weren't finding that hope in what the churches had to offer. That mission cost them both a great deal. They risked their reputations and their careers by exposing themselves to criticism and ridicule. In Conan Doyle's case particularly the sacrifices were huge. His own mission cost him what could have been a very comfortable retirement, many friends, a large fortune which he devoted to his campaigns and ultimately his health and his life. By then, however, the Church had been forced to face directly the challenge posed to its authority by spiritualism and psychical research. What should the reaction of the minister be to the medium?

Chapter 8

The Church Under Threat

Conan Doyle and Oliver Lodge had highlighted some of the main reasons why the Church's response to the carnage of the War seemed inadequate to many of the bereaved. They had offered an alternative to the "cold comfort, the windy words and the dogmatic assertions" of bishop and archbishop that Conan Doyle had criticized so scathingly. That alternative involved apparently direct communication with those who had died and personal assurances that they had survived the grave; it didn't depend on religious faith, which many of the bereaved might lack, or on the performance of religious rituals. The evidence for the survival of loved ones was available to all who were prepared to seek it.

The War had also had the effect of drawing attention to all kinds of psychical phenomena, mostly concerned with the apparent survival of men who had been killed. Raymond Lodge was far from being the only soldier allegedly communicating directly with his family, comrades and friends. It was said to be quite a common occurrence for soldiers to see apparitions of comrades who had been killed. One particularly vivid and convincing example involved the colonel of a regiment who was very popular with his men and was badly wounded, losing an arm. After convalescence he wasn't allowed to return to Flanders in a fighting role, but was sent to command a garrison in the Dardanelles; but he fell seriously ill on arrival and was immediately shipped back to England, where he died shortly after being put on to a hospital train. At the moment of his death he was apparently seen by his old comrades in their Flanders trench. They knew nothing of his death and were surprised that he had unexpectedly returned to his old regiment. He was seen by more than 100 men in different areas of the trenches, until he suddenly disappeared. Witnesses described him with his usual pair of binoculars but with both his arms. Yet news of his death in England didn't reach his regiment until the next week.

Many reports of such 'crisis apparitions' arose during the War, though this phenomenon is not limited to wartime. There have been numerous such cases reported throughout the history of psychical research and many of them have been carefully investigated. The common feature they share is the appearance of somebody at the time of their death to family members or friends. Particularly impressive are examples when it was not known that the person was dead or dying, and when those experiencing the apparition had no particular reason to expect the person's death, as was the situation with the Colonel. There were many cases of this kind reported during the War and analyzed by the SPR. A lot of them occurred not on the battlefield but back in England (Carrington, 1920).

Such incidents did not involve the participation of a medium, and seemed to show to those experiencing them that the veil between life and death was a thin one. Many bereaved families, therefore, were persuaded to follow the example of the two knights and seek direct contact with their loved ones through a medium. The evidence for individual survival of death produced from many of the most impressive cases was again closely scrutinized by the SPR.

If it was true that the veil was indeed so thin and could be pierced by anyone with the help of a medium, this meant that the Church had lost its monopoly over pronouncements about life after death that it had enjoyed for centuries. It was no surprise, then, that the growth of spiritualism and of psychical research caused such dismay among many clerics. By the start of the War, church attendance and membership had already been in steady decline for 20 years or so (Kollar, 2000). This was partly due, many felt, to the confused Anglican doctrines about death, heaven and hell. *The Book of Common Prayer* stated that the dead were no longer with us and could not be spoken to, nor even about, in any way that affected their well-being. The Protestant Church had abandoned the Catholic belief in purgatory, which offered a halfway house between eternal bliss and eternal damnation. As a result, prayers for the dead were condemned on the grounds that they had no biblical foundation: 'faith in Christ' was all that was needed for Christians to enjoy immediate fellowship with God after death. The huge loss of life during the War, however, did finally force the Church to start to rethink its theological position on this issue, and as the Archbishop's Commission on Christian Doctrine observed in 1971, "The events of the First World War marked a decisive point... and since then prayers for the dead have been widely used among Anglicans."

Another area of Church doctrine which proved inadequate in providing sufficient help and comfort to the innumerable numbers of bereaved families during the War was that concerning the so-called 'Communion of Saints'. This referred to the supposed union of all members of the Christian Church, living and dead, who were deemed to be part of the 'mystical body of Christ'. Although this belief (based not on any reported sayings of Jesus, but on St. Paul's complex theology) still features in Christian creeds, many felt it to be too obscure and confused to offer much direct consolation to grieving relatives, particularly when they, or their loved ones, may not have thought themselves qualified as 'members of the Christian Church' and certainly not as 'saints'. William Temple, later to become Archbishop of Canterbury, attempted to explain the doctrine, claiming that it could bring consolation to the believer when faced with death: "They are not lost to us. In their closed union with God we find them once more in the degree in which our own souls attain to unity with Him." If such obscure pronouncements were intended to clarify the doctrine, however, it's not difficult to understand why many trying to come to terms with the sudden loss of a young soldier blown to bits in France found the message of the medium more relevant than that of the minister.

It was becoming clear that the Church could not continue to turn a blind eye to the threat posed by spiritualism and psychical research. The Church Congress held at Leicester in 1919, referred to in the previous chapter, was the prelude to a more comprehensive debate on spiritualism at the Lambeth Conference of 1920, where bishops of the worldwide Anglican Church met. One session of this Conference considered the relationship of spiritualism to Christianity and a committee was appointed which reported later in the Conference. The growth of spiritualism in Great Britain was acknowledged, together with the threat it posed to the Church. Predictably a variety of opinions was voiced by the bishops on the subject. Some dwelt on the failure of the Church to meet the spiritual needs that the War had created. Some lamented that spiritualism, along with theosophy and Christian Science, had abandoned essential Christian beliefs and become alternative religious systems; spiritualism had thus become a 'cult', while the traditional Christian faith remained the only source of spiritual truth with the only true 'medium' being Jesus Christ. Some warned of the dangers of 'dabbling' with spiritualism, which could cause 'incalculable harm'. Some, while granting the appeal of spiritualism and the usefulness of some psychical studies, insisted on the supremacy of Christian doctrine: the first resolution produced by the committee stated that "the revelation of God in Christ Jesus is the supreme and sufficient message given to all mankind whereby we may attain to eternal life."

Was this message going to be "sufficient" for all those who did not accept the Conference and its bishops as the fount of all wisdom? Had the Church adequately addressed the challenge of spiritualism and psychical research? Had it considered whether they might complement and enrich some areas of

Christian belief? The traditional Church was struggling, whereas spiritualism was thriving. Was there no possibility of the two becoming allies, as Conan Doyle suggested, "to fight the materialism of the world"?

Chapter 9

A Church Divided

The Anglican Church leaders had recognized the threat to their authority posed by the rise of spiritualism and psychical research, but there was less agreement, as the 1920 Conference had shown, over how to respond to that threat. This was partly due to some confusion about the nature of the challenge: was it spiritualism or psychical research that had to be confronted? As we saw earlier, the two were by no means identical, differing widely in their aims, approach and ethos. Inevitably, though, there was some overlap in their interests, particularly in their focus on mediums and mediumship.

If the Church leaders wished to treat spiritualism as the target, they could try to attack it on theological grounds, as a 'cult' which was undermining the necessity for 'faith'. This involved viewing it as a new, rival 'religion', even though we have seen that this was not a claim made by Conan Doyle and Oliver Lodge, who saw spiritualism as entirely compatible in most respects with Christianity (and indeed with other religions). Moreover, this form of theological attack by the Church was unlikely to carry much weight with many who did not see themselves qualifying as 'Christians' accepting all orthodox Christian doctrines.

On the other hand, if psychical research was to be the Church's target, it was venturing on to even more dangerous ground. Psychical research didn't rest upon any religious system of 'faith' and didn't aim to prove or disprove any religious beliefs. From the start, it had simply insisted on the need for open-minded, rigorous investigation of phenomena, and it had thereby attracted the interest and attention of many eminent scientists. Was the Church to object to the spirit of free enquiry necessary for this research and to the pursuit of new knowledge and understanding? If so, wasn't this a repeat of its notorious condemnation of Galileo?

This seemed to be the position being adopted by some influential Church leaders. William Temple, the future Archbishop of Canterbury and leading Anglican theologian and intellectual, whom we met in the previous chapter, made the following remarkable declaration in a public lecture he later published (Temple, 1935):

It seems to me, so far as I can judge, positively undesirable that there should be experimental proof of man's survival of death. For it would bring the hope of immortality into the area of purely intellectual apprehension. It might or might not encourage the belief that God exists; it would certainly, I think, make very much harder the essential business of faith, which is the transference of the centre of interest and concern from self to God... I cannot ask that so-called Psychical Research should cease. But I confess I hope that such research will continue to issue in such dubious results as are all that I am able to trace to it.

It's difficult to understand how an Anglican intellectual could adopt such an anti-intellectual and anti-scientific position, but again the explanation must partly lie in that notion of a threat to 'faith', which many of the bishops at the Lambeth Conference had feared. But 'faith' in what exactly? Presumably not simply in God, because Temple distinguished "the belief that God exists" from "the essential business of faith". The 'faith' that Temple and the bishops were wanting to protect was in some of the traditional doctrines and creeds, promoted by the established Church and its representatives, yet it was those very doctrines and creeds that so many were increasingly finding it hard to accept or even make sense of. These people didn't apparently count as 'Christians' in the eyes of the Church if they didn't share such 'faith' – nor did they presumably qualify as members of Temple's exclusive 'communion of saints' which, according to doctrine, was the only link between the living and the dead and which required membership of the Christian Church.

It's easy to appreciate, then, why the Church's opposition to spiritualism and to psychical research failed to strike a chord with many. Furthermore, the Church's problems were compounded by the fact that it was not speaking with one voice on this matter. There were in fact those **within** the Church who were sympathetic to spiritualism and psychical research and who were not afraid to express their support. Bishop Welldon of Durham, for example, went so far as to invite Conan Doyle to speak on the subject, declaring that it was impossible at the current time to laugh "spiritualism out of court."

Support from the clergy also came from the Rev. Charles Tweedale, who had previously published an influential book entitled *Man's Survival After Death*. Tweedale was an active campaigner who founded a society for Christian spiritualists, the Society of Communion, to encourage psychical studies among Anglicans. He insisted that the 'Communion of Saints' must involve communion with the dead and that psychical phenomena offered the only effective means to achieve this communion. He also pointed out, as Conan Doyle did, the similarities between spiritualism and the early Christian communities. His arguments were vigorously supported by another campaigner for collaboration between spiritualism and the established Church, Mrs. St. Clair Stobart, who founded a group of clergy and spiritualists aiming to promote the essential similarities between spiritualism and Christianity. Mrs. Stobart was highly critical of the Christian churches for their insistence on doctrine and ritual, as exemplified in their pessimistic burial services and in their teaching on the nature of God, the "resurrection of the body" and the "vicarious atonement" of the

Crucifixion.

Another clergyman and colleague of Mrs. Stobart who proclaimed a similar line of argument was the Rev. Maurice Elliott. His writings and other activities finally led in 1935 to his Bishop complaining to the then Archbishop of Canterbury of his "going into the diocese around London speaking about Spiritualism". (Kollar, 2000) The Bishop had apparently prohibited spiritualist meetings being held in any of his churches, a move approved of by the Archbishop, who warned of the dangers of "spiritualistic séances and the like". This Archbishop, Cosmo Lang, will play a major part in the next chapter, while Maurice Elliott will also come to our attention again later.

An even more direct challenge to the Church's anti-spiritualist stance came from an Anglican vicar, who became one of the best-known mediums of the post-War period, the Rev. George Vale Owen. During the 1920s he was the author of a number of widely read books, containing material produced by his own automatic writing. This at first involved apparent communications from his family and friends, describing the conditions they had experienced after their death. Later, however, the messages seemed to be coming from a band of 'higher' spirits, who dealt with a much wider range of subjects, describing various aspects of spiritual development in the next world and the different stages through which progress was made.

Vale Owen's books became popular internationally and were reprinted immediately in five languages. He received many invitations to speak to audiences at home and abroad and soon came to the attention of Conan Doyle, who declared that he was the "greatest spiritual force in England". The two men became friends and Vale Owen (who coincidentally bore an uncanny resemblance to Sherlock Holmes) invited Conan Doyle to speak at his church in 1921. This invitation was readily accepted and

Conan Doyle described the vicar's "dear little church" as "a lighthouse leading them to higher and purer realms". (Owen, undated) Not surprisingly, this event did not meet with the approval of the Church authorities, and Vale Owen's bishop issued a stern reproof. This led to a storm of protest in his parish of Orford and in letters to the national newspapers. Vale Owen himself received many letters of support from his fellow clergy.

One result of this altercation was that demands for Vale Owen as a speaker doubled. After much thought, he decided that his duties as a vicar were severely restricting his freedom to pursue the cause he now felt dedicated to, and so in 1922 sent a letter of resignation to his Bishop, who no doubt received it with much relief. For the rest of his life until his death in 1931 he continued his mission by writing and lecturing, including a tour of America in 1923. Believing as he did that spiritualism was entirely compatible with Christianity and that the textbook of the Christian Spiritualist was the Bible, he helped to establish Christian Spiritualist churches throughout the country, which still exist. His high profile during the 1920s created controversy and attracted much criticism, particularly from religious quarters. One Catholic priest, for example, tried to ridicule Vale Owen's description of the afterlife, saying that he had seen the same sort of thing in Piccadilly, flashing out something about Bovril.

Vale Owen's mission represented a further serious threat to the Church's position as the sole authority on life after death. He and his supporters among the clergy were blurring the distinction between the medium and the minister, for he was showing that the same person could fulfil both roles. Church leaders could try to reject critics such as Conan Doyle as being 'anti-Church', but when some clergy were openly campaigning for spiritualism and urging the Church to recognize the contribution it might make to the question of life after death, the situation urgently called for a more positive response than the bishops had come up with at their 1920 Conference. It was at this point that the current Archbishop of Canterbury, the leader of the Anglican Church, Cosmo Lang, whom we have seen warning of the dangers of "spiritualistic séances", was forced to take action.

Chapter 10

The Report That Would Not Stay Secret

How was the Anglican Church and its anti-spiritualist Archbishop going to respond to the challenge of spiritualism and psychical research? The answer reveals an intriguing story of power politics, clashes of strong personalities, alleged cover-ups, leaks of secret information, documents filched from filing cabinets – and all this involving the higher echelons of the Church of England.

The main instigator of the whole affair was Francis Underhill, who was to become Bishop of Bath and Wells after serving as Dean of Rochester. He moved a resolution at the Church Assembly of 1935 that "in view of the growth of spiritualism among the clergy and communicant laity of the Church, the Assembly respectfully requests their Graces the Archbishops to appoint a commission to investigate the matter and to report to the Assembly." This interesting reference to the growth of spiritualism "among the clergy" underlines the point made in the previous chapter: supporters and practitioners of spiritualism and psychical research were now to be found within as well as outside the Church.

After a lot of behind-the-scenes negotiation which we need not describe in detail here, the Archbishop of Canterbury, Cosmo Lang, invited thirteen prominent Anglicans to form a committee under Underhill's chairmanship "to investigate the subject of communications with discarnate spirits and the claims of spiritualism in relation to the Christian faith." (The material quoted in this chapter is taken from *Spiritualism: the 1939 Report to the Archbishop of Canterbury*, edited by Michael Perry, 1999.) Lang didn't want a formal commission which he thought would not be "expedient" but rather "a small body to carry on quiet investigations". (Note that word "quiet"!) Three of those invited declined, and a fourth, Evelyn Underhill, a cousin of Francis Underhill, resigned with a bang after the first meeting. She spoke in her letter of resignation of the "utterly sub-Christian, anthropocentric, hopelessly unsupernatural character of the spiritualist outlook... It will be a very ill day for the Church of England, when she allows it to be assumed that she can come to terms with the spiritualist outlook. She is already too much concerned with sub-religious interests... The Church should stick to her supernatural job as the Body of Christ."

Clearly, then, there was disagreement and controversy right from the start. It also seems from the correspondence we have between Lang and Underhill that they were hardly on the same wavelength. Lang, for example, speaks at one point of the "dubious methods" of spiritualism and the dangers of "dabbling" in it (a favorite term of abuse that critics then and even now often resort to). Underhill on the other hand had actually taken the trouble to do his homework. He had researched and read widely about the subject, and had had some sittings with mediums, where it seems his parents and a former Archbishop had communicated.

The committee had its first meeting in 1936 and finally reported to Lang in 1939. It contained four parts, and its main points can be summarized briefly as follows. (The full Report can be read in the publication cited above.)

The first part lays out the origins of the committee and reports Evelyn Underhill's acid letter of resignation. Part 2 contains some introductory material which all the committee agreed with. It describes the current position of spiritualism and its relationship with the Christian faith in view of the drift towards it from some within the Anglican church. It tries to define spiritualism and asks whether it can properly be called a religion. It sets out the characteristics of various spiritualist organizations and their basic beliefs, and then gives a long list of different types of psychical phenomena and mediumship. Finally in this section there is a brief and rather confusing discussion of 'facts', 'evidence', 'hypotheses' and 'revelation', which includes the debatable claim that "neither scientific facts nor scientific hypotheses involve any questions for Christian doctrine."

Part 3 summarizes the evidence of witnesses given to the committee. These strangely were not named in the original report, but we do know now who they were, though it's not clear how they were chosen. Most of them are either spiritualists or psychical researchers, and predictably their evidence is often contradictory. The committee also attended at least one séance, but we hear very little about that. A number of interesting individual points are raised by some of the witnesses, but the overall impression is (again predictably) one of entrenched positions and irreconcilable disagreements.

After hearing this so-called evidence, the committee remained divided in its own opinions. As a result, we find in Part 4 the conclusions of the majority, followed by a minority report signed by three members. Even in the conclusions of the majority there are signs of disagreement and contradiction, or at least big differences in emphasis. This produces some inconsistencies in places, where attempts are made to try and keep everyone happy. One good example of this is where it's claimed at one point that spiritualism hasn't added anything to our understanding of Christian truths. Yet in the very next paragraph we are told that spiritualism can add a "new immediacy and richness to the belief in the Communion of Saints" and that "there seems no reason at all why the Church should regard this vital and personal enrichment of one of her central doctrines with disfavour..." It's difficult to see how those two views can be reconciled: spiritualism cannot be said to add nothing to Christian 'truths' and at the same time to 'enrich' them. There is also much said at this point about the distinctions between belief and knowledge, and between facts and faith. Spiritualism is criticized for claiming to rely on scientific verification, whereas Christian beliefs must rest upon faith. It seems in this section that spiritualism can't really win either way – either it's at fault for trying to seek scientific verification or it's at fault for not producing **enough** convincing evidence of that kind.

In fact, some of the final conclusions of the majority are quite bold. It is probably true, we are told, that some communications do come from discarnate spirits. Spiritualism contains a truth which can "fill in certain gaps in our knowledge, so that where we already walked by faith, we may now have some measure of sight as well." On the other hand, there is said to be a danger that spiritualism may have its center in man rather than in God, and that it may be a substitute for religion. However, the Church does not altogether escape criticism either; it is accused of not proclaiming and practicing its faith with enough conviction, and of being altogether too cautious in its references to the departed and in its prayers for them. These are points which have frequently cropped up in previous chapters, and which we shall return to later.

Probably the most revealing part of this majority report comes in a brief footnote to the final paragraph. That paragraph recommended that "representatives of the Church should keep in touch with groups of intelligent persons who believe in spiritualism." Yet the footnote to this reads, "The Committee do not recommend that any publicity be given to this note." The implication of this remarkable recommendation could hardly be clearer. In other words, the Church is being advised to keep in touch with those "intelligent persons who believe in spiritualism" (not the unintelligent ones, presumably!) but to keep very quiet about it. That footnote foreshadows the veil of secrecy that was to surround the Report for many years.

The minority report was signed by three members, who included a bishop's wife and a bishop's secretary. They considered that there was no evidence that spiritualists could communicate with discarnate spirits, but at the same time dismissed such communications as "valueless, misleading, dangerous, trite and banal". None of them added to "our knowledge of Christian revelation." However, at the séance attended by the Committee the authors of the minority report could "offer no explanation" of the phenomena they witnessed. Spiritualism was said to encourage "morbid curiosity" and superstition, and to lead to "diminished belief in the sovereignty of God and the redemptive power of Christ." Chancellor Garth Moore, an eminent Anglican, in his later assessment of this minority report, reprinted in the publication mentioned above, described it as being "utterly predictable and containing nothing but the familiar indictments of what its authors would no doubt have regarded as the occult."

In many respects, then, the Report resembled the curate's egg (or perhaps the Archbishop's!) in being quite good in parts. It did give an airing to some important questions and revealed some deeply divided opinions, while the majority report was open-minded and brave enough to commit itself to admitting the possible value of spirit communication. On the other hand, there is no indication of how the witnesses were chosen or how their evidence was edited. There is no bibliography or reading list of relevant literature. What theology there is in it is dogmatic and often confusing, while the overall style is in places dense and convoluted.

Perhaps the Report's greatest weakness, however, was in not distinguishing clearly enough between spiritualism and the much wider area of psychical research. As we saw earlier, that distinction was, and still is, a crucial one. The Church could try to attack spiritualism as a religion on grounds of theology, but the investigations and findings of psychical researchers needed to be considered on their merits as scientific investigations and not dismissed arbitrarily because they might challenge certain doctrines. Few Church leaders, however, seem to have been prepared to study those findings in any depth. William Temple's declaration, quoted in Chapter 9, clearly demonstrates how he, as a leading intellectual within the Church, was prepared to ignore the growing mountain of well-validated data being produced by psychical research and to hope that it would continue to issue in what he dismissed as "dubious results". Just how much investigation Temple had actually done is unclear, as is the relevance of his 'hopes' to the validity or otherwise of the "results", but much of the data becoming available at this period could hardly be simply written off in this condescending way as "dubious".

The Report was duly completed and submitted to Archbishop Lang, who clearly was not at all happy with it. In a letter to the chairman, Underhill, he said that he found it "useful and impartial", but was "somewhat disappointed" and wished that the majority report "had laid greater stress upon the dangers awaiting individuals who may be inclined to dabble in spiritualist methods." The question of ultimate publication of the Report raised "many difficult issues", and he needed to consult with the Bishops at their next meeting. This was hardly a ringing endorsement. Lang then delayed sending copies of the report to the bishops (with the words Private and Confidential, underlined and in bold type, on the front cover) until a few days before the meeting, when it was squeezed on to the agenda following a long and difficult discussion of "The Church in Time of War". The bishops decided by a large majority that the Report should not be published, and Underhill expressed his disappointment at the brief amount of time allowed to debate the issue and the fact that the bishops were tired by the preceding discussion. It was finally agreed that the Archbishop should "send a message to the Chairman of the Committee thanking them for their conspicuous service, at the same time making it clear that it was not proposed to publish their report." The higher echelons of the Anglican Church, then, had failed to grasp the nettle that spiritualism and psychical research represented.

But that was far from being the end of the affair. Although access to the Report had been closely guarded, someone blew the gaff and there was a leak. The indefatigable Mrs. St. Clair Stobart, whom we met in the previous chapter, was somehow given a broad description of the Report including the main conclusions of the majority, and this then appeared in the spiritualist publication, *Psychic News*. At this point Archbishop Lang seems to have panicked, as he asked his bishops whether they wanted to change their minds about publication. Underhill was now firmly in favor of this, saying that it "might be of assistance to many thousands who were in need of information and guidance." He was still fighting a losing battle, however, and was heavily outvoted by his fellow-bishops, including William Temple, who feared that publication would suggest that it had "the commendation and approval" of the bishops.

One might have expected that this would be the final blow to the Report and that its fate would be to continue to gather dust on the shelves of Lambeth Palace. That was not allowed to happen, however, and Lang began to receive many letters, not all from spiritualists, requesting the publication of the Report and condemning the "clerical censorship" which had caused its suppression. With wartime casualty figures mounting daily, the Church was accused of repeating its failure during the First World War to comfort the sorrowing and bereaved and of withholding the support that spiritualism might bring to many. The editor of *Psychic News* wrote: "In war-time, when religion should be able to give a magnificent lead, Orthodoxy pathetically scuttles itself. The refusal of the Primate to publish this historic document is one more nail in the coffin of Orthodoxy." (Kollar,

2000)

Criticism of the Church's handling of the Report continued throughout the war years, and Lang's replacement as Archbishop by William Temple predictably did not lead to a change of policy. Despite continuing pressure from several quarters, Temple maintained his opposition to "any recourse to spiritualistic séances and the like", declaring that only through "self-surrender to God made known in Christ could one find the real secret of eternal life." He even went so far as to rule (astonishingly) that "it would not be right for a priest to baptize an infant if one of the parents was a Spiritualist."

Temple had boasted in a letter that he "took a foremost part in urging that the report should not be published," thinking that it would be "discreditable to the Church" to produce "so amateurish a statement." He could hardly have been delighted, therefore, by yet another remarkable twist in the saga. Apparently an unknown member of the original committee felt so aggrieved at the whole affair that he invited Maurice Barbanell, the then editor of *Psychic News*, to his office, told him he was going out for an hour, and that if he were to look in a certain drawer, he might find something of interest. The contents of the drawer were finally revealed to nonclerical eyes and a copy of the majority report duly appeared in *Psychic News*. Yet even after that, successive Archbishops still continued to try and maintain the Church's official silence on the matter, and it was not till 1979, 40 years after its original production, that the full text was released and published in the journal, the *Christian Parapsychologist*.

By then, however, yet another intriguing development had taken place, which some spiritualists might claim had given them the last word on Archbishop Lang and the Report he had so unwillingly authorized. The Archbishop had died in 1945, long before the Report was finally published, but one of the most famous mediums of the period, Leslie Flint, claimed that he had been contacted by Lang over a long period beginning in 1946. Flint's form of mediumship involved directly reproducing the voices of the apparent communicators independently of his own vocal cords. He claimed to be the most tested medium ever, having been confined in boxes, tied up, sealed up, gagged, bound and held. To ensure that the voices were not coming from his own mouth, his lips were sealed with Elastoplast [bandages] and he was made to fill his mouth with colored water which he returned to the glass at the end of the sitting. No deception was ever detected over many years of testing. Many tape recordings were made and closely studied of the voices, many of which are still available on several websites (e.g. www.leslieflint.com and www.wholejoy.com/I/LeslieFlint).

The voice claiming to be Lang's was said to be identical to the former Archbishop's by a former chorister who had had frequent direct contact with him at York Minster. This witness stated that Lang's slow style of speech and many of his mannerisms came out very well on the tape and that he had every confidence that it really was Lang. If that was so, Lang had certainly changed some of his religious views. "If only I could have my life over again with the knowledge I now have," said the disembodied voice on the first occasion, "how differently I would act. I could have done so much, but I was afraid." (Flint, 1971) Later the voice admitted, "I suppose I had, in a sense, a narrow religious conviction... Many of the things that I had preached, many things that I gave out as truth... these things held me back, and still, do... Dogma and creed which were, of course, so part of my life, I realized were non-existent and unimportant here, and a man is no more after death than he was before... We can forget and discard all our creeds and dogmas." Lang also seemed to have revised his ideas about spiritualism, which he now thought was the essence of the early Church, and which was still so vital and so important that all should know about it (Randall, 1975).

Whether or not these comments really did come from Lang

after his death, they highlight some of the main religious issues where spiritualism had proved to be incompatible with the traditional creeds and doctrines of orthodox Christianity, despite the ambiguous conclusions of the Report. We shall return to these again later, but it's now time to leave spiritualism temporarily to one side and ask what was happening to the other potential threat to the Church's authority – psychical research.

Chapter 11

Mounting Evidence from Mediumship

The strange story of the 1939 Report has been told in some detail, not simply because of its historical interest but also because of the light it sheds on many of the issues that this book is concerned with and which still face anyone today trying to work out why they should or should not believe in the possibility of an afterlife. In particular, it highlighted the sharp distinction between two possible sources of information about life after death – direct communication via a medium from those who had died and religious teachings based on the Church's traditional doctrines and creeds. The Report, as we've seen, did little to resolve this conflict, or to distinguish clearly between the claims of spiritualism and the evidence offered by psychical research.

In fact, many researchers have seen the first half of the 20th century as providing some of the strongest and most convincing psychical evidence for the survival of the individual personality after death. To attempt even to summarize the best of this evidence is well beyond the scope of this book, particularly as some of the classic cases are complex and call for study in depth. An excellent, balanced review of this material can be found in David Fontana's *Is There an Afterlife?* (2005).

However, to give just a flavor of some of the remarkable results produced by some mediums during this period, which were rigorously investigated and continue to be analyzed, here is a brief sample of three famous cases. (An additional example has already been described in Chapter 5, provided by the evidence collected by Sir Oliver Lodge of apparent communications from his son, Raymond, received by several mediums and minutely dissected by Lodge in his book. This was, and remains, a further important contribution to psychical research into mediumship and survival of death.)

The Airship Disaster

In 1930 the giant airship, R101, crashed near Beauvais in France on her maiden flight to India, killing 48 of those on board. Two days after this horrific accident, one of the best-known mediums of that period, Eileen Garrett, was holding a sitting at the National Laboratory of Psychical Research in London. The specific object of this sitting was to see if a communication could be received from the recently deceased Conan Doyle. No direct contact was made to begin with, though an apparent convincing communication from Conan Doyle did occur later. But what did happen at the start of the sitting was even more extraordinary. The name of 'Irwin' was spoken, followed by a stream of technical information, conveyed in short sentences, relating to the airship and its fateful journey, for example, that the bulk of the airship was too heavy for her engines, the gross lift was badly computed, the elevator had jammed, the oil pipe was plugged, the fuel feed was unsatisfactory, the air pump had failed, the fabric was waterlogged, and the superstructure of the craft was not resilient. The pilot of the doomed airship had been Flight Lieutenant Irwin.

Further sittings were held with Eileen Garrett at which more details were given, most of which were confirmed as accurate. Other members of the R101 crew also apparently communicated, at times conveying information which was only much later confirmed as accurate. Controversy inevitably raged over the whole business, especially as 'Irwin's' comments seemed to hint at negligence and an attempted cover-up by the Air Ministry. The saga continued for many years and cannot be described in detail here. For those interested, a fascinating account of the whole affair is contained in John Fuller's book, *The Airmen Who Would Not Die* (Corgi, 1981), while an excellent, much shorter overview is given in David Fontana's book, cited above. Fontana's conclusion is worth quoting here:

> **I do not consider that anyone who comes to the strange and tragic story of the R101 with as much objectivity as we humans can muster (which admittedly may not be that much) can reach any conclusion other than that a great deal of the information given by Eileen Garrett was paranormally acquired, and that the survival of Irwin and the other unhappy officers is, on balance, the most likely explanation as to its source.**

The Cross-correspondences

The year of the R101 disaster also marked the end of a lengthy episode in the history of psychical research, considered by many investigators to constitute the most powerful evidence ever collected for the survival of the human personality. This episode, usually labelled the "cross-correspondences", took place over almost 30 years and produced a huge amount of complex material which is still being analyzed by researchers today. Whole books have been devoted to this, the most recent being an exhaustive study by Trevor Hamilton, running to more than 300 pages, over 30 of which are devoted to references and bibliography (2017). Hamilton's cautious and balanced conclusion is that some of the material shows "design, purpose, insight and self-reflection (and) a sense of continuing consciousness post-mortem." Even to give a flavor of all this is far beyond the scope of this book, and so all I shall try to do is to offer a very brief outline of this remarkable series of events, which yielded what can hardly be written off in Archbishop Temple's dismissive words as "dubious results".

By 1906 a number of the British pioneers in psychical research had died. The SPR was at that time investigating scripts produced by a number of reputable mediums, using the method of automatic writing. This involved allowing the writing hand to move of its own volition over sheets of paper, usually with the medium being unaware of the words and sentences that were appearing. This was one of the methods used by Mrs. Leonora Piper, whom we met in Chapter 4, and also by the Rev. George Owen (see Chapter 9). The SPR investigators noticed that the automatic scripts being produced by mediums working in India and the USA as well as Great Britain (described by Fontana as a most "illustrious group of Victorian ladies", of whom only one was a professional medium) had many strange characteristics. While appearing to be puzzles making little or no sense when taken individually, the scripts when put together seemed to have common themes which provided the keys to the puzzles. These themes were usually derived from often obscure references to Greek and Latin literature, a highly significant feature given that the deceased pioneers who seemed to be behind the communications had all been classical scholars. By 1912 two more gifted classicists who had examined the scripts had also died, and appeared to join forces with the original communicators in experimenting with this ingenious method of demonstrating their survival and their continuing mastery of classical literature.

Not many of us today share that mastery, which can make it difficult for us to appreciate the complexity and subtlety of the scripts, and their classical puzzles. Just a brief mention of some of the simplest examples will have to suffice here to give a hint of what the communicators were apparently trying to do.

Early on, for instance, the theme of 'death' was highlighted independently by three of the mediums in quotations from Latin, Greek and English poetry. Another case, known as "The Ear of Dionysius", made the trickiest of *Times* crossword clues look like child's-play, though it was described (optimistically) by Professor Archie Roy, an expert on the cross-correspondences, as "one of the simpler cases". This involved a variety of classical allusions, all of which suggested a connection with a grotto at Syracuse in Sicily, constructed by the tyrant, Dionysius, and known as his 'Ear' as he used it to overhear conversations of his prisoners held there. The scripts became more and more enigmatic, referring to a range of Greek myths and legends, until it was realized that all the strands of the communications came together in a highly specialized book on the Greek Melic Poets, which would have been unfamiliar even to most classicists. The apparent main communicator, however, a Dr. Verrall, had owned a copy of this book and used it in some of his university lectures.

The medium mainly involved in the production of this obscure material, Mrs. Willett, had practically no knowledge of classical literature. This was by no means her only contribution to the study of mediumship during this period. Mrs. Willett (a pseudonym, concealing her real name of Mrs. Coombe-Tennant) was no back-street medium, aiming to console the bereaved for payment. She stood for Parliament, was a JP in Wales and became the first woman appointed by the British Government as delegate to the Assembly of the League of Nations. She was also one of the mediums involved in an even more elaborate "cross-correspondence" known as the "Palm Sunday Case", extending over 30 years and considered by many investigators to offer probably the best evidence ever produced for life after death. The central character in this drama of what Professor Archie Roy described as "a remarkable demonstration of undying love and devotion by people on both sides of that inevitable appointment we call Death" was no insignificant, long-forgotten figure, but a man who was to become Prime Minister and Foreign Secretary of Britain, Arthur Balfour. Today his name is chiefly remembered in connection with the so-called Balfour Declaration, a public statement issued by him in 1917 on behalf of the British government announcing support for the establishment of a "national home for the Jewish people" in

Palestine. The following is a very brief summary of his moving and complex involvement in the cross-correspondences.

Arthur Balfour met and fell in love with Mary Lyttleton in 1871 at the home of William Gladstone. Just before he was about to propose to her, however, she fell ill with typhus and died on Palm Sunday, 1875. Balfour arranged that she should be buried wearing an emerald ring of his mother's and also had an engraved silver box made specially to hold a lock of Mary's hair. Subsequently Balfour never married and every year thereafter kept Palm Sunday as a special day of remembrance for his lost sweetheart. His interest in psychical research later led to him becoming President of the SPR and so being aware of the growing amount of material associated with the cross-correspondences.

It was not until 1912 that it was realized by the investigators that for many years scripts had been produced by various mediums, including Mrs. Willett, with many phrases, symbols and drawings which had made no sense at the time, but which now could be seen to apply directly to Balfour's long-lost love. These were as numerous as they were ingenious, including, for example, references to the Palm Maiden and Palm Sunday, May blossom (Mary had been known as May), King Arthur, locks of hair and a box with engravings of periwinkles, as Balfour's box had been. As was a common feature of the cross-correspondences, these were often communicated through literary allusions.

The breakthrough came about in 1912 when Mrs. Willett produced an automatic script in the presence of Arthur Balfour's brother, Gerald, as requested by the communicator, who declared, "Look back. Far back I come. Years ago I have been beating at the door. Shall I ever reach him?" It still took the cautious Arthur Balfour a further four years to have a sitting with Mrs. Willett, which produced more references to May, May blossom, Arthur and a lock of hair and other significant allusions. Arthur Balfour is reported to have found all this "disturbingly meaningful", and only then revealed the facts about the lock of Mary's hair in the silver casket, which were unknown to all those involved in producing the scripts. His final conclusions about life after death were summarized in a letter to a friend: "For myself I entertain no doubt whatever about a future life. I deem it as least as certain as any of the hundred and one truths of the framework of the world... it is no mere theological accretion... death cannot long cheat us of love." (Roy, 1996)

Swan on a Black Sea

The third representative sample of evidence for life after death produced by mediums during this period and closely scrutinized by psychical researchers also involves Mrs. Willett, but in a very different capacity. The medium involved this time was Geraldine Cummins, perhaps the most celebrated practitioner of automatic writing in the history of psychical research, and the communicator was apparently the deceased Mrs. Willett herself.

Geraldine Cummins bore no resemblance to the typical image of a medium. She was an Irish author, playwright and international hockey player. She described herself as "a normal individual... quite the reverse of the eerie, exciting, neurotic, screaming individual many people conjure up in their imagination as the character of the sensitive or medium who experiments in psychical research."

The material that Geraldine Cummins produced through automatic writing over a period of 30 years or so covered a wide range. The earliest examples purported to be narratives of early Christian history from immediately after the death of Christ and seemed to be independent of the Biblical record. They contained much factual material that was entirely unknown to Cummins and which was judged to be accurate by several leading theological scholars, including professors of Hebrew and Divinity. For example, the head of the Jewish community in Antioch was quite correctly named as "Archon", though this was a newly introduced title, which only a specialist in the period would have known about. The scripts were written at great speed usually without pause or correction, whereas Cummins was normally a slow and laborious writer.

A later set of scripts was allegedly communicated by someone we have already met several times, Frederic Myers, who had died in 1901. These contained detailed and complex accounts of the afterlife in language characteristic of Myers when he had been alive. Geraldine Cummins had never met Myers, but his old friend, Sir Oliver Lodge, accepted the scripts as genuine and dealing with subjects and ideas they had once discussed. Myers' widow also endorsed the scripts.

The most convincing evidence for life after death produced by Cummins, however, came later from a different and unexpected source. This was the lady who was the subject of the previous section, Mrs. Coombe-Tennant, who had featured prominently in the Palm Sunday Case under the pseudonym of Mrs. Willett, as we've seen. She had died in 1956 and Cummins was unaware of her true identity; she also had had no personal acquaintance with her or her family. Cummins was contacted by the SPR to see if she would try to obtain a message from an SPR member who had recently lost his mother. Unknown to Cummins, this was Mrs. Coombe-Tennant's son. She agreed, and over the next two and a half years produced 40 scripts, which have since been closely analyzed and assessed for their accuracy. They contained a vast number of facts and references, much too detailed to be described here; a whole book has been devoted to them, *Swan on a Black Sea*, with a lengthy Foreword by the eminent Cambridge philosopher, Professor C.D. Broad (Cummins, 1966).

Initially, before Cummins became aware of who the communicator might be, the scripts focused on demonstrating the survival of Mrs. Coombe-Tennant by providing a wealth of specific information about herself, her family, friends and past life. This included the name of herself and her children, her life in Wales and her work as an "automatist" with "the Cambridge group", and as a magistrate. In later scripts the communicator, having established her identity and her survival of death, engaged in a critical self-analysis of her life, character, relationships and failings, emphasizing the learning experiences that had occurred after death. Many investigators who have studied this material have concluded that any attempt to explain the scripts in terms of coincidence or fraud is much more incredible than the possibility that Mrs. Coombe-Tennant really was communicating from beyond the grave, or as Geraldine Cummins herself put it in a typically cautious question, "Is there a swan (a soul) that rises from the Black Sea of Death and flies away to other regions?"

These examples of mediumship, it must be again emphasized, represent a minute fraction of the data produced by psychical research in the UK and in many other countries, available for public scrutiny during the period that the Church of England Report lay unread on the shelves of Lambeth Palace. They have been selected to show that the results of mediumship research by this time could hardly be airily dismissed as "dubious", as William Temple had tried to do. They also illustrate how the evidence for life after death was not limited to what was offered in spiritualist churches, but was subject to examination and assessment by scientists, theologians and philosophers. However, the gulf seemed as unbridgeable as ever between religious and psychical claims to provide answers to questions about life after death. Could some sort of reconciliation ever take place between the medium and the minister?

Chapter 12

The Experience of Colonel Lester

We've now seen a number of attempts to bridge the gap between religious and psychical approaches to the subject of a life after death. Most of these, however, were undertaken at an individual level, sometimes by clergymen such as Vale Owen and Maurice Elliott, who were prepared to stick their ecclesiastical necks out and risk incurring the wrath of the established Church, sometimes by psychical investigators such as Oliver Lodge, who saw no necessary incompatibility between the two approaches. Yet at an institutional level there had been little sign of a meeting of minds. The Church, the SPR and the various spiritualist organizations still viewed each other on the whole with suspicion and at times with outright hostility. There existed no organization dedicated to trying to reconcile the opposing viewpoints in a constructive way.

This situation was now about to change, not through the initiative of a minister or a medium, but of a Lieutenant-Colonel, who had fought in both World Wars and had not found traditional Christian doctrines a satisfactory response to the slaughter he had experienced. As a result, he was skeptical of the whole idea of life after death, an attitude which was further strengthened after the Second World War when in 1948 his wife to whom he was deeply attached suddenly died. This man, Reginald Lester, who had become a prominent journalist, later described the crippling sense of bereavement he then suffered, to such an extent that he contemplated suicide. "Here was the supreme occasion in one's life when comfort was so greatly needed," he wrote, "and the Church was completely unable to supply it." (Lester, 1952) In line with many of the critics quoted in earlier chapters, he found that the clergy were "extraordinarily vague" about what happened after death, relying on "outworn dogmas" and "wishful thinking as the only foundation of the faith (they) preached." What this generation needed, he argued, was "a religion that will appeal to their reasons as well as their hearts... Knowledge must take the place of a vague faith."

Lester decided that his intense grief left him with two options. Either he could attempt to rejoin his wife by taking his own life, or he could pursue an "intensive investigation" into the possibility of life after death to see if there was any scientific, provable basis for it. When on the point of taking the first option, he received a phone call out of the blue from an old friend of his wife's, who asked him to contact Air Chief Marshal Lord Dowding, the man credited by many as having done more than any other individual to win the Battle of Britain, and indirectly thereby the Second World War, by his role in overseeing RAF Fighter Command. Lester had never met Dowding, but reluctantly agreed to write to him immediately. A meeting was arranged at which Dowding told of his own research and experiences with mediums, about which he had written several books. Lester, who described himself as a confirmed skeptic with a lifelong prejudice against any form of psychical research, was nevertheless sufficiently impressed to discard his first option of suicide (which Dowding convinced him would not achieve the result he wanted), and to undertake his own exploration of the whole subject and the strength of the evidence.

His book, *In Search of the Hereafter* (1952), tells in detail how he proceeded to do just that over the following three years. The book describes his firsthand experiences with the best-known and best-reputed mediums he could find. He approached these sittings critically and analytically, examining all possible alternative explanations for the results produced. In this way he finally reached what he called "the final and true deduction, which was not only the logical one, but also founded on a scientific basis." He was, then, far from being a gullible sitter, having built up what he described as "a wall of disbelief" and a highly suspicious attitude over many years of reasoning.

At his very first sitting with a medium, to whom he was a complete stranger, he found his skepticism being challenged. Detailed information was produced referring to his wife's appearance and her wedding ring. Could the medium have been using some form of clairvoyance to get these results, he wondered? A second private sitting with the same medium provided much more evidence. Lester was taken through a remarkable resume of their 27 years of married life and his army service, with not one incorrect item, sometimes reminding him of events he had forgotten about. He came away from the sitting with "a surprising sureness that all that had happened was just what it purported to be," and some of his friends felt that he had received more than enough evidence to dispel all his doubts. His obstinate skepticism wasn't going to give up without a fight, however, and he decided that only an accumulation of evidence from different mediums could give him the conviction that he was seeking.

So began his long program of investigation involving a wide variety of mediums, using different methods of contacting those who wished to communicate. These methods included automatic writing, physical materializations and 'direct voice', where it is claimed, as with Leslie Flint, that the communicator's voice can be produced independently of the medium's vocal cords. Lester sampled all these phenomena with his usual cautious skepticism. He judged some of the mediums to be dubious and even fraudulent, while others continued to impress him with the evidence they provided of his wife's survival. Finally in 1951 came what he called the climax of his investigations, when he experienced a range of physical phenomena within a group sitting. "The evidential value was as high as any phenomena that can be achieved," he commented.

The accumulated evidence that Lester had gathered over this period forced him "by its clear logic and hard facts" to reverse his earlier position of disbelief. He was now quite convinced that, as he put it, "life is continuous; that we shall undoubtedly meet our loved ones again when our jobs on this earth are completed... and that communication between the two worlds is now a scientific fact and one of the great essential truths, the knowledge of which we are in duty bound to spread throughout this present bewildered world." This declaration was remarkably similar to those made by Oliver Lodge and Conan Doyle at the start of their mission a generation earlier, but Lester's mission was to take a very different form from that of his predecessors.

Chapter 13

A Fellowship to Bridge the Gulf?

How was Lester going to spread his message? His first step was to set to work on a book to publicize the evidence he had acquired and the comfort it had brought. This knowledge he felt it his responsibility to pass on to the world in general. His book, *In Search of the Hereafter*, from which the above quotations have been taken, was published in 1952, and anyone reading it today cannot help but be impressed by the cautious, hard-nosed attitude it reveals.

Lester was probably not expecting the immediate reaction that followed the publication of the book. He received 800 letters of support and enquiry, many of them (perhaps surprisingly) from clergy and ministers of all denominations. Many of these said that they accepted the truth and importance of Lester's findings, but were afraid to refer openly to the subject for fear of incurring the disapproval of their bishops and their congregations, no doubt for the reasons we've explored in earlier chapters. Other letters came from many lay people who could gain no comfort from their church, which they felt would disapprove of any psychical activities, including mediumship.

The best way to break this vicious circle, Lester decided, was to try to form some organization within the churches themselves to study the whole subject. He therefore contacted a number of leading clergy whom he knew were likely to be sympathetic, including the Rev. Maurice Elliott, who has appeared in an earlier chapter and whose wife was in fact a medium. A first meeting was held in November 1953 where it was decided to send a letter to *The Times* describing the proposed organization, to be known as *The Churches Fellowship for Psychical Study*, and inviting applications for membership. The stated aim of the

Fellowship was to "encourage the study, within the Churches, of the known facts of Psychic Science."

Lester and his colleagues didn't anticipate the response they would get. For several weeks applications poured in at the rate of a hundred or so a day, and Lester and Elliott found themselves burning the midnight oil trying to deal with them. Many of them came from people who said that they had never before taken an interest in the subject. No opposition came directly from the Churches themselves, though one highly significant incident showed that antagonism and suspicion of any psychical activities was still very much alive and kicking in some official ecclesiastical quarters. The *Church Times* refused to mention the new Fellowship in its columns or to publish a letter from its Committee. The paper's editor, however, in view of the wide press publicity elsewhere that was being given to the Fellowship, finally published an article attacking it from an anonymous 'Catholic Expert'. No right of response was allowed except a letter to the correspondence columns, which was drastically abbreviated and followed by another hostile comment from the 'Catholic Expert'. This was followed by an adverse editorial and the suppression of all letters commending the work of the Fellowship. One can only imagine what the reaction of Conan Doyle and Oliver Lodge would have been! Lester himself commented how "misconceived prejudice" still existed in some quarters, resulting in "a leading organ of the established Church (making) every effort to keep the fundamental truths from its readers."

The early history of the Fellowship and its later development has been described in detail by Barbara Bunce in a book, *So Many Witnesses* (1993), and does not need to be repeated here. A few points, however, are of particular interest and significance for our investigation.

The Fellowship's membership grew rapidly, reaching over

a thousand within a year. Full members had to belong to a recognized church, but associate membership had no such requirement. Branches were soon set up all over the country, conferences were held and regular publications produced. Officers were appointed to administer the various activities, and by 1956, 26 Vice Presidents had been appointed, half of them clergy including four bishops, one dean and five canons. Although from the start it was emphasized that the Fellowship aimed to study psychical matters "within the Churches", this didn't mean that membership was limited to clergy or to one particular denomination; one early active member, for example, was Dr. Leslie Weatherhead, a leading Methodist with a high public profile. By 1960, the Fellowship could claim the support of twelve current bishops and two retired ones in their list of members and officers. Clearly a number of influential clergy were showing much more enthusiasm for psychical studies than did their pre-war predecessors. This enthusiasm, however, does not appear to have been shared by the then Archbishop of Canterbury, the leader of the Anglican Church, who stated in what sounds like a coded warning to the Fellowship that he was "eager that the CFPS should be a body such as would commend itself to the Church and command the confidence of church people."

In 1963 the Fellowship voted to change its title to *The Churches Fellowship for Psychical and Spiritual Studies*, which it has retained to the present day (CFPSS). This reflected growing tensions within the organization and demands to broaden the Fellowship's areas of interest. Spiritual healing, for example, had been a particular interest of Reginald Lester's and a source of some disagreement from the start. Some influential early members also wanted to put the subject of mysticism on the agenda, while others wished to emphasize that psychical research investigated a far wider range of phenomena than those involving a possible life after death.

It was this last issue of evidence for an afterlife that created and continued to create what Barbara Bunce in her history of the Fellowship called "the greatest minefield to be negotiated – the area of mediumship." This was inevitable in view of the Fellowship's declared affinity to "the Churches" and their history of suspicion and hostility towards the role of mediums as intermediaries between the living and the dead. Despite the Fellowship owing its inception to Reginald Lester's loss of faith in orthodox Christian doctrines and his willingness to test rigorously what mediums had to offer him following his bereavement, tensions between the Fellowship's Psychical Research Committee and the more traditional Christian elements among the membership were never far below the surface, at times leading to what Bunce described as "accusations of prejudice and of being controlled by the ecclesiastical hierarchy." Lester himself went so far as to declare in a later book that "the one obstacle that had been preventing the spread of spirit communication (was) the prejudice of the orthodox Churches."

The creation of the CFPSS, then, had not removed the problems arising from the potential conflict of the medium and the minister. In the early days, Reginald Lester's personal experiences with mediums had led to the establishment of the Psychical Research Committee specifically to investigate mediumship. This was chaired by the Rev. John Pearce-Higgins, who was to become the Vice-Provost of Southwark Cathedral. An experienced and enthusiastic investigator and member of the SPR with close contacts with leading mediums, he took every opportunity to publicize their activities in his writing, lecturing and participation in public debates, sometimes on television. Mediumship, then, was far from being a subject of embarrassment to the early leaders and members of the CFPSS, as it tended to become later. One member who was destined to become a bishop, Mervyn Stockwood, went so far as to invite a well-known medium, Ena Twigg, to speak at the University Church in Cambridge in 1958, when he was a Canon there. Another famous medium, Ursula Roberts, demonstrated her gifts at the Fellowship's Annual Conference of 1960. Reginald Lester invited Ena Twigg to the Fellowship's annual dinner, introducing her by declaring that the cooperation of experienced Spiritualist mediums was invaluable.

This open acknowledgment of the significance of mediumship, however, later became a source of controversy within the Fellowship, as a number of leading figures used their influence to encourage more orthodox Christian doctrines and to discourage the earlier endorsement of mediumship. The Rev. Martin Israel, a dominant figure within the CFPSS as Chairman and President during the 1970s and 1980s, in one of his many books, *Life Eternal* (1993), wrote that mediums needed to be "people of devout prayer", and that he regarded "with less enthusiasm their attempts to bring fellowship between the deceased and their loved ones still on earth." In words strongly reminiscent of William Temple's, which we noted in an earlier chapter, he claimed that direct proof of personal survival would "severely blunt the cutting edge of faith by which we grow spiritually."

Israel's successor as Chairman and President, Canon Michael Perry, was equally influential and even more cautious in his attitude towards mediumship. Even a single sitting with a medium following a bereavement "has its dangers," he wrote, "and ought not to be enterprised without careful Christian counsel." Instead, his advice to the bereaved was that "help can be given by their religious faith and through the pastoral counsel they receive from the clergy or Christian friends." (Perry, 2003) Such help and counsel was hardly sufficient for the CFPSS's founder, Reginald Lester, as we've seen, but Perry, despite being a long-standing member of the SPR, declared that the Fellowship was "solidly grounded within orthodox Christianity", and that while it did not "forbid resort to mediums", such a course was a "spiritual cul-de-sac". (Perry, 1992) This was a far cry from Lester's charge that the prejudice of the orthodox Church "prevented the spread of spirit communication".

These quotations show how far the CFPSS had moved towards traditional Christian orthodoxy since its inception. Mediumship was grudgingly acknowledged, but its alleged (undocumented) dangers were being stressed rather than the potential good it might produce. It should never, a later CFPSS leaflet stated, "seek to disturb the communion of saints, but rather let them take the initiative." Even the words 'medium' and 'mediumship' tended to be avoided where possible, in favor of the much vaguer terms 'sensitive' and 'sensitivity'. Religious faith was the answer to bereavement, rather than psychical evidence.

The history of the CFPSS, then, vividly illustrates how difficult it has been to negotiate that "minefield" that Barbara Bunce referred to (above). It had not managed to bridge the gulf between the medium and the minister, though it had and still does play a valuable role in drawing attention to the psychical element in Christianity and the overlap between religious and psychical questions. This also opened the way to the development of a new area of study with its own substantial literature, including the publication of the Fellowship's journal, the *Christian Parapsychologist*, which is still produced and widely distributed.

The CFPSS, however, was not the only organization to focus on the relationship between religious and psychical issues. In 1965 two Unitarian ministers, George and Florence Whitby, founded the Unitarian Society for Psychical Studies (USPS), which like the CFPSS continues to this day. George Whitby was a distinguished academic, holding posts at Glasgow and Sheffield Universities. He was also a prominent member of the CFPSS and of the SPR. As with several other figures we've already met in this book, Whitby's involvement in psychical studies and afterlife investigations arose partly from his personal experience of family bereavement. In 1963 his son, Roger, was drowned in a diving accident at the age of 21. Whitby later wrote how "within six months he was communicating with us through professional mediums and telepathically through his mother." These communications, dealing mainly with Roger's experiences after his death, were published in a book entitled *Gateway*, which has been recently reissued with additional material about the USPS (Whitby, 2015).

The USPS has numbered many prestigious members and supporters in its ranks, including a number of academic professors in various disciplines. Dr. Robert Crookall, whose research will be described in the next chapter, served as Vice-President, and Sir Alister Hardy, a pioneer in the study of mystical and religious experience and a President of the SPR, was a life member.

It's not surprising that Unitarians should have been willing to explore the relationships between religious and psychical studies and to take the work of mediums seriously. Unitarianism believes in a rational approach to religious exploration and embraces many world-views. Though essentially rooted in the Christian tradition, it is free from the restraints of creeds and dogmas. This means that psychic experiences can be viewed open-mindedly and assessed on their merits. The USPS has not felt the need, therefore, to conform to orthodox Christian beliefs in the way that the CFPSS often has.

Another religious group which, like the Unitarians, is not committed to orthodox Christian doctrines and which contains members willing to explore psychical areas is the Quakers or Society of Friends. The Quaker Fellowship for After-Life Studies (QFAS) appeared on the scene later than the CFPSS and USPS, being founded in 2000 specifically to study "ideas and evidence concerning life after death". Their publications and conferences have often focused upon mediumship, without the reservations expressed by the CFPSS.

Before we finally leave the CFPSS and the tensions it generated, though, we need to look at a more dramatic clash between the psychical and the religious approaches to the afterlife, in which two characters already mentioned in this chapter played an important part: the minister, John Pearce-Higgins, and the medium, Ena Twigg. The main personality involved in this extraordinary saga, however, was an American Bishop, accused of heresy and destined to die prematurely in the Judaean desert.

Chapter 14

The Curious Case of the Heretical Bishop

The conflicts between the medium and the minister which we've been exploring were evident on both sides of the Atlantic. At the center of the most sensational example of the controversies that resulted, soon after the founding of the CFPSS, was a colorful character whose experiences attracted wide publicity and heated debate.

Bishop James Pike was a minister of the Episcopalian Church, a mainline Christian denomination and member of the Anglican Communion: in effect it was, and is, the North American version of the Church of England. He was appointed to the prestigious post of Bishop of California in 1958, and soon started to ruffle ecclesiastical feathers as a result of his (then) unorthodox views on various topics. Pike was in many ways ahead of his time, taking a liberal position on political, racial and sexual issues, and using the media to reach a wider audience. Theologically, he also supported the ordination of women, but it was his challenging of some traditional Christian doctrines that led to him being accused of heresy by members of his own Church, though he never faced a formal trial.

He set out his views forcefully in a number of books. In *A Time for Christian Candour* (1964), for instance, he claimed that many Christians were "bogged down by too many doctrines, mores, precepts, customs, symbols and other traditions," and were confronted in almost every Church by "a complex series of doctrinal propositions, an extensive set of do's and don'ts, an elaborate structure of government and relationships, a thick holy book of diverse materials... and a complicated scheme of public worship." He attacked fundamentalist approaches to the Bible, as expressed in the evangelist hymn, *Jesus Loves*

Me, This I Know, For the Bible Tells Me So. "But what proves the Bible?" asked Pike. "The Bible is not self-evidently final or self-authenticating."

Several of the Church's key doctrines also came under fire. Many people had been put off Christianity, he argued, by the Church's proclamation of the Virgin Birth narratives as both history and dogma, despite the fact that they are not mentioned in the earliest Christian writings, the Epistles of Paul and Mark's Gospel, nor in the later gospel of John. Another line of his attack was against the doctrine of the Trinity and the language in which it has been expressed, which he described as confused and unintelligible, particularly to "outsiders", but also to many an "insider". He underlined his point with a humorous recounting of a priest's experience when ministering to a man who had collapsed in a store. "Do you believe in God the Father, God the Son, and God the Holy Ghost?" asked the priest. The man opened one eye and said to the bystanders, "Here I am dying, and he's asking me riddles!"

He defended his beliefs further in typically trenchant fashion in another of his books, which threw down the gauntlet to the traditionalists with its title, *If This Be Heresy* (1967). Among his targets were the creeds, "confessions" and liturgies which featured so prominently in church services. "A mere look at various items in the present Prayer Book," he declared, "would require non-affirmation or doubt on the part of the average sensible person." Many members of the Church "when confronted with this portion or that readily enough express disbelief, doubt or diffidence."

Although Pike's criticisms aroused the ire of many traditionalists, such 'heretical' views would probably cause much less of a furor today. Many theologians, scholars and clerics (including some Bishops) have more recently voiced similar doubts, making his books seem less provocative to readers today. Yet one chapter in *If This Be Heresy* does explore ideas which would still be thought surprising to emanate from a Bishop. That chapter is particularly relevant to the issues we're investigating, as it's entitled "Life After Death".

In this chapter Pike discusses the close links between beliefs about the afterlife and about religion generally. He notes that a conviction about life after death is one of the first major beliefs to go for most people when they "jettison a conventional authority-based scheme of doctrine." Many fear death, he wrote, because it is seen as the absolute end of one's conscious existence as a person, while others may have no doubts about an afterlife, yet still dread the possibility of having to suffer a Hell of eternal torture. Not even those who believe themselves 'saved' are completely free from this fear as they may have miscalculated their chances of salvation. Pike's irreverent sense of humor comes to the fore again here as he mocks the Catholic teaching that anyone receiving Holy Communion or Mass "in a state of grace" for nine consecutive first Fridays of the month would be guaranteed ultimate entrance into heaven – no matter what happened in their earthly life thereafter. "One would think," he wrote sardonically, "that a modicum of efficiency with reference to one's date book and alarm clock could thus dispose of the fear of hell. But not so. The haunting fear remains." Perhaps, he continued, a mortal sin might have been omitted in the confessional box, or genuine repentance was not present, or an "impure thought" had been forgotten about and not confessed, and so on.

Yet our belief in an afterlife need not, according to Pike, be based upon dubious religious grounds. His study of psychical phenomena had led him to reach similar conclusions to those of Sir Oliver Lodge when he declared:

Persistent existence is a fact (and) occasional communication across the chasm – with difficulty and under definite conditions – is possible. The evidence

has thoroughly convinced me (1) of human survival, (2) of the possibility under favourable circumstances of communication between the dead and the living, and (3) that death is only an episode in a continuous existence... The evidence is cumulative, and has broken the back of all legitimate and reasonable scepticism.

Pike goes on to underline his agreement with Lodge by giving examples of the evidence that had most impressed him. As a result, he was prepared to maintain that "personal survival of death is a fact, and that 'what' survives is identifiable and unique, and represents a new phase in the existence of the person." In addition, what we know about personal, psychological development strongly suggests that our personal survival of death must involve the freedom and opportunity to grow. This makes impossible, he insisted, the conventional Christian doctrine that one's fate is settled as of the moment of death – a heaven of infinite bliss or a hell of infinite torment. Quite apart from any theological or moral considerations, this contradicted plain facts about the nature and functioning of persons. Credible instances of afterlife communications also suggested that there were opportunities after death for growth in knowledge, awareness and maturity. All the evidence, then, pointed to the nature of personal life after death being of the same essential character as personal life now.

There was for Pike, therefore, a clear factual basis for his belief in personal survival. This was a startling claim for a Bishop to make, when most senior clerics would have been expected to base such a belief on religious faith. However, the impact his arguments would have made (if any) on the general public paled into insignificance in comparison to the reactions that another book produced, for this was not a weighty theological work but a sensational account of Pike's own psychic experiences and explorations following the death of his son Jim.

This book was entitled *The Other Side* (1969). It told a lengthy and complicated story and quickly attracted enormous publicity and controversy, which Pike didn't seek to avoid. The saga began in 1966 in Cambridge, UK, where the Bishop was spending a six-month sabbatical, accompanied by his son. Jim had been beset with a number of psychological problems, exacerbated by his addiction to drugs, but had seemed to benefit from the short study course that he had taken at Cambridge. However, shortly after returning to resume his university course in San Francisco, he took his own life, shooting himself in a hotel room in New York.

After dealing with the necessary arrangements at home, Pike returned to Cambridge with two assistants to resume his program of research and meetings that had been so tragically disrupted. The three of them used the same apartment that Pike and Jim had shared earlier and immediately started to be confronted with a strange series of bizarre events. Books, postcards and pictures were found in unexpected positions, the two assistants had disturbing experiences at night and the hands on Jim's alarm clock seemed to have been changed to the time at which he would have taken his life. Other weird phenomena occurred, leading Pike to speculate that Jim was somehow responsible for what was going on. Feeling that he needed advice from someone familiar with such matters, he contacted a fellow-clergyman whom he knew slightly and who has already appeared in our account of the CFPSS, Canon John Pearce-Higgins. This resulted in the Canon arranging a meeting with the best medium he knew, Ena Twigg.

Pike gives a full account in his book of this first sitting, during which the medium claimed to be in contact with Jim, enabling his father to have a lengthy conversation with him. Pike seems to have been impressed with the sitting and with much of the material that was communicated, though it was not clear how much prior information Ena Twigg would have had about the Bishop, whose public profile was high on both sides of the Atlantic. Towards the end of the sitting she did, however, produce a highly convincing piece of evidence, not from Jim, but from an academic friend of Pike's who had recently died, the well-known German theologian, Paul Tillich. He apparently communicated in a German accent and thanked Pike for dedicating his latest book to him. Ena Twigg could hardly have known about this as the book had only just been published. Pike arranged another sitting with Ena Twigg before returning to America, during which he asked 'Jim' how he could contact a medium in the States, should he want to do so. The reply was, "Spiritual Frontiers – a Father Rauscher – priest of the Church – in New Jersey."

On resuming his diocesan duties, he was preaching at a church in New York City when he was told that a minister wished to speak to him after the service. This man turned out to be a well-known medium, the Rev. Arthur Ford. He told Pike that he had seen a figure standing behind him with the name of Jim and that he (Ford) was connected with a group called the Spiritual Frontiers Fellowship, whose president was a Father Rauscher of New Jersey. Then, following a complicated series of what Pike interpreted as meaningful "coincidences", he had another sitting with another medium associated with Spiritual Frontiers, the Rev. George Daisley, who again claimed to make contact with Jim.

By this time Pike's career had taken a further turn. While still facing a heresy trial by Church authorities, he resigned as Bishop of California in order to concentrate on his academic work, including his forthcoming book, *If This Be Heresy*. His psychical explorations also gathered pace with further apparently meaningful "coincidences" and with sittings with George Daisley, all of which he describes in detail in his book. His personal life also continued its tragic pattern, when one of his close associates, who had been with him in Cambridge and with whom he may have become emotionally involved, herself committed suicide.

Despite all these pressures, Pike then agreed to go ahead with a TV appearance that was inevitably going to create considerable controversy, admitting (somewhat naively) that he had failed to realize that "it would draw national – indeed international – news coverage." The idea was for a program featuring Pike, a chairman, Allen Spraggett, and a medium, who would discuss psychical questions before the medium would try to go into trance and transmit messages. The medium involved was the Rev. Arthur Ford, who had spoken to Pike after the New York City service. Ford apparently managed to make contact with Jim and a number of other names who had had connections of some kind with Pike. Much of the information and names produced could conceivably have been researched by the medium in advance, but Pike later wrote that this would have had to be done "in a most elaborate and sophisticated way." The séance lasted two hours and Pike seemed to have been impressed overall.

The reactions to this program coincided with further developments in the heresy saga, and Pike had not, it seemed, been prepared for the sensational newspaper headlines that appeared, such as "Bishop Pike's Talk With His Dead Son". Reporters then besieged him with phone calls and Pike admitted that he had "demonstrated a distressing lack of foresight" which had created the image of "a credulous, bewildered and grieving father desperately seeking to absolve himself of guilt by claiming to have been in communication with his dead son."

Mail flooded in, mostly positive but some hostile attributing Pike's experiences to "the work of the Devil". Others based their criticism on their belief that the dead remain asleep until the last Judgment Day. He even had an invitation to preach at one of the largest Episcopal churches withdrawn, as the rector said he did not want people coming to the service "just because they might hear some sensational revelations." Some other comments were less restrained, such as "This time Pike's really gone off his rocker!"

Pike defended himself at length against these and other comments in his book. He also considered the suggestion that he had been taken in by a very clever plot, devised by all or some of the people who had been involved in his explorations, and that he was being used in this way by spiritualists and mediums to "carry their banner". Resenting the implications of credulity on his part, he decided to review the whole saga so far and try to assess whether such a plot was conceivable. His conclusion was that it was highly unlikely and would have required a complicated conspiracy to achieve. He conceded that fraud on the part of George Daisley, Allen Spraggett or Arthur Ford was theoretically possible, though his "personal, intuitive assessment" and "genuine respect" for these men told against this. He therefore arranged a further private sitting with Ford, which he claimed completely allayed any theoretical concerns about his integrity. However, serious doubts were later cast upon Pike's assessment, when Allen Spraggett in a book about Ford published after his death claimed that he had discovered a substantial amount of evidence in Ford's papers that strongly suggested detailed prior research on his part, enabling him to produce information to offer to sitters.

One further sitting with Ena Twigg is described in Pike's book, which followed the usual pattern of apparent conversation with Jim. This provided no specific evidence that it was indeed Jim communicating and was largely concerned with general theological matters. Interestingly, some of the comments voiced were probably not in line with what Pike would have wanted to hear, and so could not be explained in terms of the medium picking up material telepathically from the sitter. For example, in answer to Pike's question, "Have you heard anything over there about Jesus?" he was told, "Oh, it is difficult. I'm afraid

I might hurt you... People must have an example... They talk about him – a mystic, a seer. Oh, but, Dad, they don't talk about him as a saviour... not a saviour, that's the important thing – an example."

Pike's book appeared in 1969, but later that year he finally hit the headlines in yet another dramatic turn of events. While pursuing his research into the origins of Christianity, he was travelling with his newly married third wife in Judaea. He rashly undertook a risky car journey into the desert, unprepared, on which they became lost and marooned. His wife set off on foot for help, but the rescuers returned to find that he had left the vehicle and had disappeared. For several days no trace could be found of him and it was not known if he was alive or dead.

At this point the two people whom we have seen were involved in Pike's initial forays into the psychical domain reentered the story – the medium Ena Twigg and the minister John Pearce-Higgins. Ena was contacted by Pike's wife to see if she could get some clue as to the bishop's whereabouts. She had no immediate success, but some days later, when Pike's fate was still unknown, she held a taped sitting with Pearce-Higgins and her husband. She was unaware at first of what transpired as she was in trance, but the two sitters later told her that Pike had communicated and had clearly died. She could not bring herself to listen to the tape immediately but played it the next day.

The transcript, reprinted in her autobiography, *Medium* (1973), makes fascinating reading. The communicator, if indeed it was Pike, appears to be deeply troubled and appealing for help, having choked to death in the sand. Pearce-Higgins tries to reassure him, emphasizing that a sudden death is often followed by a short period of confusion and disorientation. "This may take three days," he tells Pike. "It took Jesus three days to come back, didn't it?" "But I'm not Jesus," replies Pike. "But it's a process that happens to everybody," counters Pearce-Higgins, "... this happens to anyone who dies suddenly." "But not to a bishop!"

complains Pike indignantly. Pearce-Higgins is understandably irritated by this, retorting, "Oh, blow you, a bishop! You are just a human being." Pike gradually becomes less disturbed, telling Pearce-Higgins that he is a great comfort, but he is worried that his son hasn't come to help him. Pearce-Higgins repeats that it is too soon. "Haven't you read your Crookall?" he asks, referring to research that will be described in our next chapter. Pike again seems to lose his cool, exclaiming, "Baloney!" to which the ever-patient Pearce-Higgins replies, "Baloney... All right, brother... you know..." The lengthy conversation finally ends with Pike expressing concern about his next unfinished book not being published and his ring not being found. Pike's widow later confirmed that the tape contained enough references that corresponded to the circumstances of their ordeal and to issues that she knew had been uppermost in her husband's mind at the time to allow her to affirm that he had indeed been communicating through the medium.

Pike's experiences and investigations, however, continued to be the focus of heated controversy long after his death. Several books were published on the subject, including a lengthy, critical biography of the bishop, and doubts persisted about the honesty and motives of some of the mediums involved. These books fueled further heated exchanges; one review of the biography, for example, called it "an amalgam of vulgarity, innuendo and malicious gossip."

But this is not the time or place to try to assess Pike's reported experiences after 50 years have now elapsed. The reason for putting him in the spotlight in this book is because the affair is another stark illustration of what can happen when medium and minister interact. Whether one believes that all or some or none of the Pike saga was psychically based, it is still very revealing for the purposes of our investigation, showing how the two alternative approaches that can be used to base one's belief in an afterlife upon, the religious and the psychical, can easily clash and create conflict.

This is largely because the belief itself and the reasons for holding it often form part of a wider belief system and set of assumptions. Antagonism can result when it is felt that this whole system is under threat. This can most easily happen when those holding firm religious views are reluctant to accept that their 'faith' in life after death may not be the only route to reach such a conviction. The psychical approach then becomes the target for attack and aspersions may be cast upon the character, motives, trustworthiness and even sanity of those who adopt it, particularly if they are also seen to hold unorthodox religious beliefs. On the other hand, it is also quite possible for those convinced of the psychical 'proof' for survival of death to condemn some members of the 'religious faith' group as blinkered and doctrinaire. Such reactions from the opposed camps were evident in the case of Conan Doyle's campaign, which we examined in Chapter 7.

The Pike affair clearly demonstrates all this. As with Conan Doyle, the clash was probably further exacerbated by Pike's strong personality and his apparent penchant for confrontation. No doubt his (at the time) unorthodox views on some traditional Christian doctrines, which had led to the heresy charges, were a major factor in the hostility aroused by his psychical claims and his readiness to publicize them. It seems significant that many of the professional clergy who have been most sympathetic to the psychical approach have also tended to hold a 'liberal' theological position, allowing them to be critical of some traditional aspects of the Christian faith. Two of the eminent Anglican clerics, for example, whom Pike had contact with, Canon John Pearce-Higgins and Bishop Mervyn Stockwood, certainly came into this category, as did a later Bishop who was to write extensively about psychical issues, Hugh Montefiore. None of these men was a stranger to controversy and all were prepared to consider open-mindedly the results produced by mediums and the evidence this could offer for life after death.

Chapter 15

Learning More About Mediumship and the Afterlife

We've seen in Chapter 10 how the Church of England, under pressure from the spread of spiritualism, had reluctantly felt the need to instigate the ill-fated 1939 Report, which eventually reached the public domain in 1979. This lack of enthusiasm for the whole subject of psychical communication continued, with no attempt on the part of the Church to review or revise its often confused teaching about life after death. Perhaps the authorities felt that this was hardly a priority in view of the steady decline in Church membership and the increasing workloads of its clergy; its time and energies seemed to be devoted more and more to such issues as women priests and bishops, homosexuality, same-sex marriages and allegations of child abuse. It's arguable, however, that these issues were (and are) of less concern and interest to most members of the public than the question of what, if anything, might face us all after our inevitable physical death.

Fortunately, while the Church and orthodox Christianity may have largely washed its hands of the subject, this attitude was not shared by the two movements which had first threatened its monopoly as the authority on all things concerning life after death – spiritualism and psychical research. In fact, significant developments in the study and practice of mediumship have continued to take place up to the present day.

The last 50 years or so have seen a growing awareness among the general public of what mediums do, or claim to do. Witnessing the work of a medium used to be mainly the preserve of committed spiritualists or specialist psychical researchers. Nowadays mediumship is publicized in all sorts of ways and there can be very few who haven't a rough idea of what it involves. Some TV channels have regular programs showing mediums at work, drama series are based (sometimes very loosely!) on the activities of mediums, celebrities recount their experiences of mediums, the popular press often features articles on the subject and many Internet websites are devoted to it. Mediums, in other words, have hit the media.

This tendency to portray mediumship as a form of public entertainment has developed alongside the emergence of 'star mediums' who perform at 'demonstrations', often in front of large audiences at theatres and other venues. Some of these also perform regularly on TV and are the authors of best-selling books. On a smaller scale, less well-known mediums offer their services at 'Psychic Fairs' (or 'Fayres'!) alongside other psychic practitioners specializing in such areas as clairvoyance, Tarot readings, crystal healing and so on. Many of these will also advertise for clients online and in the local press.

All this means that the public is far more *au fait* with psychical goings-on than it used to be. It's simply so much easier to sample what's on offer than it used to be. This has been a mixed blessing in many ways. On the one hand, there is less mystique surrounding the practice of mediumship and less embarrassment about showing an interest in it. On the other, this higher public profile hasn't necessarily improved the overall quality of mediumship or lessened the skepticism that many people have always felt towards it. The history of mediumship is full of instances of (and allegations of) fraud and deception, which have understandably tarnished the image of mediums generally. This hasn't been helped by the way that mediums have usually been presented in books, films, plays and on TV: it's unusual to come across a medium here who isn't fraudulent or deranged – sometimes both. Either they are confidence tricksters, plotting to defraud the gullible in various ways, or they are deluded eccentrics sitting in the dark, trying to 'raise the spirits' and enquiring (usually in a quavering voice), "Is there anyone there?" Anyone who has had even the slightest acquaintance with real mediums will know that this is a laughable caricature, but it's not surprising that it persists, given the at times dubious history of mediumship and the way it is often still portrayed today.

Has this increased public interest in and exposure to the whole business of mediumship been matched by further serious study of the subject by psychical researchers? Although psychical research, or parapsychology, has steadily broadened its scope since its early concentration on the evidence for life after death, mediumship has continued to offer investigators plenty of opportunities to assess its validity and explore its implications. Disagreement has continued between those parapsychologists who consider some at least of the evidence to be compelling and those who maintain that all of it can be 'explained' in ways that do not involve communication with the dead. There are many comprehensive books describing this evidence and the arguments on both sides (e.g. Fontana, 2005), and again for our purposes here we need only to sample very briefly the large amount of relevant material available. We shall do this by picking out just three examples of afterlife and mediumship research which illustrate different methods and approaches.

1. The Geologist who mapped the Afterlife

Dr. Robert Crookall was an unlikely candidate as a pioneering explorer of the afterlife. A distinguished geologist and botanist, he became a university lecturer before being appointed as Principal Geologist in the Department of Scientific and Industrial Research at HM Geological Survey of Great Britain. He specialized in coal-forming plants, helped in the search for coal-bearing areas and wrote the standard work on the subject, *Fossil Plants of the Carboniferous Rocks of Great Britain* (which need not concern us further here!).

On his retirement Crookall probably decided that he had devoted enough of his energies and his professional career to coal and fossil fuels. He now had time to turn his attention to a lifelong interest in psychical research and the possibility of an afterlife, but his approach was to remain true to the spirit of science. His methods were almost as fascinating as his results, which he presented in more than a dozen books and many more articles during the 1960s and 1970s.

Crookall was not concerned to test the powers of particular mediums who claimed to relay information from those who had died. In fact, his data didn't come just from mediums but from a much wider range of sources, including reports from subjects still living of so-called 'out of the body experiences' and what are now labelled as 'near-death experiences', which we shall look at in more detail in the next chapter. His approach was to gather together and compare a vast amount of material coming from a broad variety of different sources, without trying to assess the validity of any one individual report. He then looked for similarities and dissimilarities in these accounts, and like the good scientist he was, he suggested hypotheses and models consistent with this extensive database.

There is far too much of this material to try even to summarize it in any detail here, but it's difficult to read his work without being impressed by the cumulative weight of the evidence he presents, particularly relating to the conditions apparently experienced soon after death. His work never became as well-known to the general public as it deserved to be, probably because his style of writing and presentation didn't make his books an 'easy read', though they were highly influential among many serious students of the subject, including members of the CFPSS and of the Unitarian Society for Psychical Studies of which he was a Vice-President. The significance of his research has been endorsed by an eminent philosopher of religion, Professor Hugo Meynell, who emphasized the key point that each of his references would individually carry little weight, but in combination with one another seem extremely impressive to any reasonable person. Meynell concludes that it seems impossible to explain away Crookall's findings on the basis that he is either lying or deceived by his sources, and considers that another point to be made in favor of his conclusions is that they do not fit very neatly with any conventional religious view.

So what were these conclusions? Crookall developed his own technical (and at times confusing) terminology, which makes it difficult to present a straightforward summary. Briefly, however, by combining and comparing the hundreds of accounts he had gathered of "out of the body experiences", "near-death experiences", and "after death experiences", together with some mediumistic material, he deduced that we all are comprised of four "bodies", which he referred to as a physical body, a semi-physical body or "vehicle of vitality", a soul body and spiritual body. Soon after death the first two of these separate (the "second death") and are discarded, allowing a period of sleep or rest before the "soul body" enters "paradise conditions"; later comes the "third death" when the soul body is shed, having served its purpose, and we enter "true heaven conditions" via our spiritual body.

Obviously the latter stages of this process are more difficult to get clear evidence for than the earlier ones, and the most convincing aspect of Crookall's work is where he focuses on the actual experience of physical death and what is described as immediately following it. Here his scientific method of seeking similarities and differences in the accounts and proposing likely explanations of these produces some fascinating and original results. For example, he finds that those who meet a natural death as a result of extreme old age or after a long illness enter into a period of sleep, which may be deep and prolonged, while those who have been energetic and alert show no tendency to sleep. Those who die suddenly or violently are 'awake' at once and are usually confused as to what has happened. As Raymond Lodge put it, "They don't believe they have passed on."

Another common feature of experiences following physical death, Crookall found, is a form of 'judgment' involving a review of our past deeds and the effects of these, good and bad, on others. In this way we are able to share and receive back all the pain and pleasure we may have produced. This process is not described in terms of external, divine punishment, inflicted by an authoritarian God, as traditional religion has often portrayed it, but as a form of self-judgment which gives us a chance to acknowledge our mistakes and atone for them. This is necessary before we can make further spiritual progress and move on to a stage or level that we are best suited to and which is largely determined by the kind of life we have lived. "This conception," Crookall comments, "is quite lacking in sentimentality, quite free from any idea of 'pie in the sky'."

Crookall's conclusions supported a number of spiritualist beliefs. The seven basic principles of spiritualism, for example, included "the continuous existence of the human soul", "personal responsibility", "compensation and retribution here or hereafter for all good and evil deeds done on earth" and "eternal progress open to every human soul." Some of these clashed with traditional Christian doctrines which maintained that 'salvation' was dependent not on one's 'good and evil deeds', but on belief in the undeserved 'atonement' of sins brought about by the historical death of Jesus Christ. Also the 'judgment' that Crookall's witnesses described did not involve a final, irrevocable verdict by God leading to eternal damnation or bliss. Nor did any of these accounts hint at divine disapproval of communications between the living and the dead.

Crookall's aim wasn't to bolster spiritualism or to attack orthodox doctrines, however. As an experienced and distinguished scientist, he simply gathered his data from wherever he could and drew his conclusions accordingly. He described his methods as first assembling the facts, then classifying them, then suggesting how they could best be explained. This meant that his research was significantly different from those psychical investigators who were more concerned with testing the claims and procedures of individual mediums and the evidence they might produce of a particular person having survived physical death. The evidence that Crookall amassed he likened to "travellers' tales", accounts relayed by a wide range of explorers who are trying to convey a flavor of the conditions and environments they have experienced to those who are unfamiliar with them. These accounts were obviously not going to be identical, any more than descriptions of a foreign country in guidebooks are identical, but the differences were as important for Crookall as the similarities.

2. Testing the Mediums

Psychical researchers ever since the founding of the SPR and ASPR have used more conventional methods than Crookall's to investigate mediumship. Again a whole book could be devoted to this work, but just a couple of recent detailed studies will be mentioned here.

One common criticism of mediumship has been that the information they transmit can be explained in ways that don't require the cooperation of the dead. Some of this, it's been suggested, might be attributed to chance guesswork, or to the medium picking up clues from the sitter or deliberately eliciting it. Alternatively, it has been claimed that the information is usually so general that it could apply to anyone and is not uniquely relevant to the particular sitter.

A number of research studies have been conducted to test these claims in recent years, including some undertaken by academics at British and American universities. Professor Archie

Roy of Glasgow University, who has been quoted in earlier chapters, devised a series of studies with a colleague, Patricia Robertson, a university colleague with considerable experience of mediumship. These studies, which were progressively refined and made as watertight as possible, involved ten mediums and two groups of subjects. Both groups were given the same information by the mediums, but these messages were intended only for the members of one group (the 'recipients'), and not for the other (the 'non-recipients'). In later studies, the medium and sitters were isolated from each other to prevent clues being picked up, the intended recipient was identified to the medium only by number, and the subjects didn't know which group they belonged to. It was found that members of the 'recipient' group accepted far more of the messages intended for them than did members of the 'non-recipient' group, and that the odds against these results occurring by chance were about a million to one (Roy and Robertson, 2001 and 2004).

At about the same time at the University of Arizona, Professor Gary Schwartz, a psychologist and psychiatrist, began a series of experiments with mediums. In one of these a single sitter who had suffered a number of bereavements had sittings with five mediums. No visual contact was allowed and the sitter could respond only with a 'yes' or 'no'. Overall, 83% of the mediums' statements were accepted as correct. The odds against chance guesswork here were calculated in a further experiment, where non-mediums were used as a control group, at ten million to one. In another experiment a telephone connection was used under the control of the experimenter, but no conversation was allowed between the sitter and the medium, who could not even hear any response from the sitter. The sitter in advance had 'invited' a number of deceased people to make contact. The four people 'invited' were all correctly named by the medium, along with the name of the sitter, a dog and other detailed information. The odds against the medium correctly giving, as she did, six names, one initial and one relationship to a specific sitter were estimated at 2.6 trillion to one. These and other experiments were reported and analyzed in great detail in articles published in academic journals and in Schwartz's book, *The Afterlife Experiments* (2002).

3. Evidence from a Cellar

The research outlined above followed different patterns from the more traditional methods of investigating mediumship used by earlier researchers, particularly when mediums were claiming to produce so-called 'physical phenomena', which seemed to contradict the accepted laws of science and were therefore labelled 'paranormal'. Such phenomena, which had often been associated with the practice of mediumship right from the birth of spiritualism at Hydesville, could take many forms, such as the production of lights and knockings, the movement of tables and other items, and the playing of musical instruments. These phenomena didn't necessarily offer direct evidence of the survival of particular persons, whereas other forms of physical mediumship claimed to use the mysterious substance of 'ectoplasm' to build up recognizable materializations of figures who had died and even voice boxes to reproduce their voices.

Physical mediumship has always been controversial as it's particularly vulnerable to accusations of trickery, which have certainly been confirmed in many cases. Psychical researchers have therefore expended much energy and ingenuity in their testing of these phenomena, and the history of the SPR is full of detailed case studies of this kind. Such investigations had tended to become less common, as indeed had the practice of physical mediumship itself, but the whole subject reemerged into the limelight 20 years or so ago through the activities of the so-called 'Scole Group'.

This small group came to the attention of the SPR as a result of the extraordinary results they seemed to be getting for the regular experimental sittings they had been holding in a cellar in the Norfolk village of Scole. Three highly experienced researchers, including two professors, undertook to investigate the matter and held many sittings with the group from 1995 to 1998. This led to a weighty SPR publication of 300 pages, *The Scole Report* (1999), describing in great detail what the investigators had witnessed. A more digestible account, aimed at a more popular readership, was also provided in a book by Grant and Jane Solomon, *The Scole Experiment* (1999). This huge amount of material and its analysis obviously cannot be repeated here, so again the briefest of summaries will have suffice.

The Scole Group was comprised of four regular members, including two mediums. The sittings were apparently regulated by a 'spirit team' consisting of a variety of named communicators. Their stated aim was to bring about spiritual enlightenment by providing firm evidence of a spirit world and its concern for humanity. This evidence was designed to focus mainly upon physical effects inexplicable by the current laws of physics, rather than more traditional 'spirit messages'.

A very wide range of phenomena was witnessed by the investigators under conditions of tight control during 31 monthly sessions, which were also attended at times by other researchers and specialists. Points of light, for example, would appear around the room, landing on the table and on the hands of the investigators, seeming to pass through solid matter, through water, through crystals and even on one occasion through the body of an investigator. No apparatus could be found to explain any of this.

Materializations of various kinds occurred – of hands which could touch the investigators, of robed figures and faces, and of physical objects such as coins and newspapers. The coin was produced apparently to settle a bet between an investigator and a member of the 'spirit team', while the newspaper proved to be a 1944 copy of the *Daily Mail* with no sign of ageing or yellowing, yet printed on the type of paper used at that time.

Music was produced from a tape recorder from which the microphone had been removed, using a blank tape supplied by the investigators. Images appeared on cassettes of unused film again supplied by the investigators and placed by them still in their tubs on the table. The resulting pictures included some of First World War soldiers and airmen and a view of St. Paul's Cathedral. Other sealed film cassettes produced a variety of symbols, diagrams and poetic extracts (all shown in colored photographs in the *Report*).

These physical phenomena were the most dramatic form of evidence associated with the Scole Group, but the members of the 'spirit team' also appeared to communicate information and messages of a less tangible kind. The investigators were impressed by the consistent characters and personalities of the individual communicators, who seemed to be "highly intelligent entities, consistently friendly, courteous and patient... and strongly motivated by their desire to prove survival." (Fontana, 2005)

They were able to engage in lengthy conversations with the investigators, often on erudite subjects. Some messages also claimed to come from deceased SPR members in the form of puzzles referring to SPR publications.

The Scole investigation came to a sudden and mysterious end when the group announced that they had been told by the 'spirit team' that some 'interference' was being experienced and that it would be dangerous to continue the sittings. The investigators had no option but to accept this unexpected development, which was disappointing to everyone concerned. However, a huge amount of material for scrutiny and discussion had by then been gathered and *The Scole Report* covers this as well as the actual data.

As might be expected, the *Report* attracted much criticism and skepticism, both from within and outside the SPR. Much of this attempted to show that some of the controls and equipment used in the investigations were not 100% watertight and might in theory have been tampered with. However, in practice no hint of deception was ever detected by the many researchers who witnessed the phenomena, and the maneuvers needed to defeat the controls would not have been feasible in view of the layout of the cellar and the seating arrangements. In fact, a professional magician with long experience of mediumship, James Webster, attended three sittings and testified that no leading magician could duplicate the effects he had seen. In addition, the Scole Group had no incentive, financial or otherwise, to go to such unimaginable lengths in order to deceive the investigators.

The three examples described in this chapter are merely a brief sample of more recent research into mediumship and afterlife research, but they show how the increased public and media interest in the subject has been matched by efforts on the part of psychical researchers to subject the results achievable by mediums to a wide variety of rigorous investigations and testing techniques. It would be a mistake though to assume that mediumship was the **only** means of establishing apparent contact with those who have died, or the only challenge to have emerged to the Church's role as the authority on the matter of life after death. Mediumship necessarily is dependent on a third party acting as an intermediary between the living and the dead, and there may be many reasons why people are reluctant or unable to seek out such an intermediary. In the next chapter, then, we'll look at several different ways in which communication with the dead and information about an afterlife may be possible without the involvement of mediums – or ministers.

Chapter 16

Who Needs a Medium?

Can communication between the living and the dead (if it's possible) take place only via a third party – an intermediary or medium? We've already come across some examples where a third party doesn't seem to be necessary, such as the well-documented cases of 'crisis apparitions', where a person who has recently died or been killed appears to a friend or family member, who is often unaware that the person is no longer alive. There have also been many reports of people close to death appearing to be 'visited' by dead family members, who seem to be preparing them for their imminent passing and offering reassurance; such 'visitors' are always joyfully received by the dying, who are able to see them clearly and converse with them. Let's now look, then, in more detail at some other examples where mediums have not featured.

The GP Investigates

One unexpected example of apparent communication not involving mediums was explored in the research of Dr. Dewi Rees, which like so much work in this area has not received the recognition and publicity that it deserves (Rees, 2010). While practicing as a family doctor in mid-Wales in the 1970s, Rees was planning to study the medical problems associated with bereavement. During the pilot study, he was surprised by how many widows and widowers spoke of contact and continuing relationships with their dead spouses. As there was no previous information on this in the medical literature, he changed the focus of his research to investigate the nature and frequency of the experiences he was hearing about.

Rees contacted almost 300 widowed people in his area.

Of these 48.8% reported having had "some perception of, or contact with" their dead spouse following their bereavement, and 36.1% stated that this awareness remained as an ongoing process. It occurred in clear consciousness and was never sought. The experiences took different forms, sometimes visual (e.g. "He was passing through the gate"), sometimes auditory (e.g. "I hear him saying, 'I'm alright, Mary'"), sometimes even tactile (e.g. "I have felt him touch my shoulder"). The frequency was the same for widows and widowers, and was not affected by age, cultural or religious background, personality type or mental health.

This research was published in the prestigious *British Medical Journal*, which led to other surveys being conducted in other parts of the UK, in the US and in Iceland. These produced amazingly similar results to Rees's study: in Iceland again about half of the widows and widowers contacted had experiences of their dead spouse, while in the US 47% of young widows in Boston reported being in contact with their dead husbands, and in North Carolina 46% of widows interviewed felt their husbands were still with them. These statistics, like those quoted in the mediumship studies in the previous chapter, show how strong the evidence for communication between the living and the dead can be for anyone prepared to look at it seriously.

Reports from the Frontier: Near-death Experiences

There are other occasions of a different kind when the bridge between the living and the dead seems to be crossed without the aid of a medium. Rees's research is unfortunately hardly common knowledge, but most people today will have heard of so-called 'near-death experiences' (NDEs). The term has now entered our everyday vocabulary and is sometimes loosely and confusingly used to refer to any close brush with death, rather than the much more specific phenomenon that many researchers have turned their attention to in recent years. Forty-two scientific studies, for example, were published between 1975 and 2005, and there have been many more since, with an academic journal now devoted entirely to the subject. Type in 'near-death experiences' on *Google* and you'll get over eight million results – so the following brief account is far from comprehensive!

When a person has stopped breathing and their heart has stopped beating, they are considered clinically dead, but modern resuscitation methods mean that they can sometimes be revived. Despite the absence of any brain activity in such patients, some report that their consciousness has persisted during this period, and these reports show a number of consistent features. These include the experience of being painlessly separated from the physical body and being able to view it, the people in the sick room and the emergency procedures being employed. No alarm is felt and the person is guided by helpers, often through a tunnel towards a bright light (or 'Being of Light') which exudes peace, love and calmness. Relatives or friends who have previously died may also be seen. A review of the person's life may then take place before they are told they have to return to their physical body as they still have work to do on earth. Their return is usually reluctant, but the whole experience is often life-changing and results in losing all fear of dying. However, NDEs are often much more complex and variable than this very brief sketch suggests and need not contain all of these typical features.

Although NDEs have become familiar to the general public in recent years, there is nothing new about the phenomenon. Reports of such experiences from those mistakenly thought to have died go back at least to Plato well over 2000 years ago, while modern psychical research accumulated many such cases before the actual term NDE was coined in the 1970s. We've seen in the previous chapter how Robert Crookall used reports of these experiences in his research.

The close scrutiny received by NDEs in recent years has led many to argue that they represent the most convincing single area of evidence for survival of death. There has been much debate about other possible explanations of the experiences, such as the influence of drugs or oxygen deprivation. These have been countered, however, by some medical and psychological specialists, who maintain that the lucid, coherent accounts reported in NDEs are quite unlike the confused hallucinations resulting from the other suggested causes. The wider significance of NDEs is that if they really show that our consciousness is not dependent on a functioning brain and body, that consciousness may well be able to survive the final death of our physical bodies; the mind and brain will not be identical, as the materialist claims.

From the particular perspective of this book, NDEs underline and clarify several important points of special interest. For example, they suggest that we don't need a medium or a minister to gain possible information about a life after death. Also, there is no indication that those reporting NDEs have any special psychical or religious qualifications. Nor do NDEs support traditional Christian doctrines. Our consciousness appears to continue uninterrupted and there is no hint of a 'long sleep' (or even a 'resting in peace') prior to a final 'Judgment'; the 'life review', sometimes reported, usually takes the form of a guided, supportive form of **self-judgment**, not an authoritarian, external process leading to a verdict of eternal bliss or damnation.

The 'Being of Light', commonly reported, seems to take a variety of forms, depending on the belief system of the reporter (or lack of it): so while some (though not all) convinced Christians may 'see' Christ, others may 'see' alternative figures of particular religious or spiritual significance to them. Even confirmed atheists, such as the Oxford philosopher A.J. Ayer, have reported 'Beings of Light'. Ayer suffered a cardiac arrest while in hospital in 1988 and was 'clinically dead' for four minutes. After being resuscitated, he told his consultant of his encounters with "a Divine Being" and with "the ministers of the universe", adding, "I'm afraid I'm going to have to revise all my various books and opinions." He later tried to retract these statements (perhaps out of embarrassment), but his friends and family noted that after his experience he had "a kind of resurrection" and became "so much nicer".

Because NDEs can present another form of challenge to the Church's monopoly as the authority on what happens after death, they were predictably dismissed or condemned by some ultra-orthodox Christian writers when they began to be publicized. An American doctor, Maurice Rawlings, suggested that they were a Satanic ruse designed to lull us into a false of security, while Levitt and Weldon also pointed to devilish involvement, designed to "undercut and counterfeit what God has established... If there is a way to relax people away from a natural fear of death, the enemy will find and use it... The biblical explanation of death is very clear... Either the individual is taken to be with God or he is not forgiven and is taken to the future home of the devil." Canon Michael Perry, a conservative voice within the CFPSS mentioned earlier, quotes the above writers apparently with qualified approval (1984), claiming that the pleasant nature of most NDEs tempts us into "untheological optimism" and that "many Spiritualists have not so much as begun to consider the gravity of sin." It's not clear, however, why Perry wishes to tie NDEs closely to spiritualism, or why he ignores the key spiritualist principles of "personal responsibility" and "compensation and retribution here or hereafter for all good and evil deeds done on earth."

NDEs then have provoked rather desperate reactions from some religious writers to preserve traditional doctrines about sin, hell and the devil in the face of apparently contrary evidence. This is strange, because not all accounts of NDEs describe attractive, desirable conditions immediately following death. A small number of so-called 'negative' NDEs of a frightening kind have been reported. Some of these involve an assisted return to the body because the prospect of death is unwelcome; some are told that all they have previously learnt about an afterlife is false; while others claim to have witnessed distress and suffering without themselves experiencing it. Various possible explanations have been offered for these 'negative' experiences, which seem to be heavily outnumbered by 'positive' ones. Perhaps an intense fear of death and what might follow it is responsible in some cases. Many spiritualists also believe that the conditions we experience initially in the afterlife are strongly influenced by the sort of life we have led and the level of spiritual maturity we have reached; if that level is very low, we may automatically gravitate to a similar level after death in the company of others who have the same lessons to learn. Some 'negative' NDEs may offer a brief glimpse of this, possibly as a warning of the importance of our earthly lives. The frequent mention in NDEs of some form of self-judgment is also compatible with this explanation, but again it must be emphasized that the evidence from NDEs does not support any kind of decisive judicial process resulting in eternal bliss or damnation. The problem of how to investigate and assess accounts of afterlife conditions will be tackled in our concluding chapter.

NDEs offer another slant, then, on our search for evidence about the possibility of life after death, a slant that does not require the involvement of mediums or religious authorities. Two other approaches which are also independent in this way have emerged in recent years. They have not yet attracted the public attention that NDEs have, but both hold the promise of producing relevant data in new and exciting ways which invite scientific study. Let's next look at these briefly in turn.

EVP and ITC: A Multi-Media Approach?

If communication with those who have died is indeed possible, why should a human medium of some kind always be necessary to achieve this? Most communication in the modern world doesn't require face-to-face contact, nor even pen and paper; we use various forms of technology to do the job. Might similar methods be devised to allow interaction between the living and the dead?

Over the past 50 years or so, this idea has intrigued many researchers, who have experimented with all kinds of electronic equipment and techniques in attempts to contact the dead. This has produced a whole new area of psychical research, which has been labelled as Electronic Voice Phenomena (EVP), and more recently as Instrumental Transcommunication (ITC). As has often been the case in this book, there is just too much complex material here to be summarized adequately, and a very sketchy sample will again have to suffice. A good overview of the field is available in a book we've already referred to, *Is There an Afterlife?* (Fontana, 1995). Fontana's account carries particular weight as he had extensive personal experience of the subject.

In view of the negative reactions we've often found in traditional religious quarters to methods of trying to contact the dead, one would not expect much enthusiasm from the church authorities for this kind of research. It's surprising, then, to learn that it stemmed initially from the findings of two Italian Roman Catholic priests in the 1950s, who were working on tape recordings of Gregorian chants. They were hampered by the frequent breaking of the tape, which drove one of the priests in exasperation to call on his dead father for help. When playing the tape back, they heard not a Gregorian chant, as expected, but the voice of the priest's father saying, "Of course I'll help you! I am always with you." Understandably, the two priests were somewhat shaken by this and felt that they should report the incident to the Pope. His response was a welcome contrast to the attitudes of Anglican church leaders to psychical research that we've noted in previous chapters. Instead of resorting to the usual 'explanations' of delusion, deception or diabolical interference, the Pope reacted positively to the priests' report, suggesting that using an electronic machine in this way might initiate a new scientific study for confirming faith in the afterlife.

Since then, the development of EVP and ITC has involved many different approaches and types of equipment. Recording machines have been widely used, often with microphones and loudspeakers, to obtain apparent responses to specific questions and requests, and the resulting tapes have been subjected to intensive testing to establish if the voices produced could be explained by other, non-psychical means. One popular method has been the recording and playing back of 'white noise', the hissing sound heard when a radio is not tuned into a specific program or transmission. The resulting voices on some tapes have caused much controversy over how they should be interpreted. Other approaches to EVP and ITC have involved the building of specialist electronic devices; instructions for the design and operation of one of these (named the 'Spiricom') were claimed to have been communicated by a deceased scientist, Dr. George Mueller.

Another form of equipment, devised by Hans König, a consultant electroacoustic engineer, used four generators producing sound above the range of human hearing. This was demonstrated live on *Radio Luxembourg* and was supervised by the station's own technicians. One of these asked questions during the live broadcast and received answers in a clear voice. The program's presenter, clearly shaken, told listeners, "I swear by the life of my children nothing has been manipulated. There are no tricks. It is a voice from where it comes." (Quoted in Fontana, above.) He subsequently wrote a book about his experiences. König continued to demonstrate impressive results with his equipment, which was rigorously tested by physicists and communication experts, who found no evidence of fraud.

A different approach has been developed by Dr. Anabela Cardoso, a Portuguese diplomat who served as Consul General in the USA. She now edits a journal devoted to ITC research, the *ITC Journal of Instrumental Transcommunication Phenomena*. While experimenting with recordings of 'white noise' and recording a question on tape, she unexpectedly received an immediate answer from one of the radio sets she was using. She continued to ask questions directly to the radio and recorded the results, which continued to produce clear communications from different individuals, including family members, mainly in Portuguese but also in other languages spoken by Dr. Cardoso. These messages often offered evidence of individual survival, as well as information about conditions in the afterlife; one communication emphasized that a medium was not necessary for EVP/ITC to be possible. David Fontana tells of how, while observing Dr. Cardoso and inspecting the equipment being used, he asked without warning if the communicators could repeat a phrase of his choosing, such as, "Hello, David," or, "How are you?" In reply, he heard first an indistinct sentence in English, followed clearly by the words, "Hello, David. How are you?" The same test was repeated successfully on a later occasion. Some of the voices recorded by Cardoso have been shown to have acoustic features not present in human voices.

Other researchers claim to have received paranormal visual images through TV equipment. Different methods appear to have been successful, the simplest being to videotape a normal TV channel and play back sections of the tape very slowly. In this way one experimenter has produced images showing a close resemblance to various deceased members of his family, as vouched for by independent observers.

This sample of EVP/ITC research, though very superficial, at least suggests that modern technology may be able to make a significant contribution to research into the possibility of life after death in a way that does not require the participation of a human medium. The methods so far developed to do this have been necessarily quite complicated in the equipment and procedures used, and accordingly are somewhat beyond the reach and experience of most people. The final 'non-mediumistic' approach to be looked at in this chapter does not depend on that kind of specialist work, though it has come into prominence through the chance discoveries of a different kind of expert – a clinical psychologist.

Healing the Trauma

Dr. Allan Botkin was an experienced American psychotherapist specializing in grief counselling and post-traumatic stress disorder, particularly with Vietnam War veterans. In his work he had for a number of years been using a therapeutic technique developed in the 1980s, known as eye movement desensitization and reprocessing, or EMDR. This involves the patient watching the therapist's hand movements while keeping the head stationary and moving the eyes to the left and right while concentrating on a disturbing thought, feeling or image, which is 'reprocessed' by the sets of eye movements. The technique was found to uncover past traumatic events that had been repressed or partly forgotten, but was less successful in helping the patient resolve the experience. Botkin tried developing this method by getting the patient to focus on the "core of grief" at the root of the traumatic experience, which he believed was associated with feelings of profound sadness and guilt. He found that his refined method was effective in addressing these 'core' feelings.

Botkin was totally unprepared, however, for his next discovery, which he describes in his book, *Induced After Death Communication* (2005). One day he was treating a Vietnam veteran named Sam, who had suffered a horrific experience during the war from which he had never recovered. Sam had developed a close relationship with a young Vietnamese girl called Le, whom he planned to adopt and take home to America. Before he could do this, however, orders arrived that all orphaned children were to be sent to a distant orphanage. While being loaded on to a truck they came under enemy fire and Sam discovered Le's bloodstained body lying on the ground. This event caused a deep psychological trauma in Sam which persisted long after his military service. According to Botkin, he rejected the daughter he later fathered and spent 28 years isolated from his family in the basement of his home.

Botkin tried his modified EMDR treatment on Sam and noted that his grief increased and then lessened as more eye movements were done. Then, after closing his eyes, suddenly and quite unexpectedly he smiled and giggled. "I saw Le as a beautiful woman surrounded by a radiant light," he said. "She seemed genuinely happier and more content than anyone I have ever known. She thanked me for taking care of her before she died. I said, 'I love you, Le,' and she said, 'I love you too, Sam,' and she put her arms around me and embraced me. Then she faded away." He was convinced that he had just communicated with Le.

Botkin was puzzled by Sam's response, as in all his years as a therapist he had never witnessed such an immediate transformation in a patient. He was in for further surprises, as the very next day the same thing happened with another Vietnam veteran, Victor. His trauma had resulted from seeing his best friend, Charlie, killed in a gun battle. For years he had been haunted by the image of Charlie's bloodstained body. Like Sam, after closing his eyes during the EMDR treatment, he smiled and told Botkin, "I saw him, Charlie. I guess it was his spirit. He looked very happy and he had a big smile."

Within three weeks Botkin had witnessed six similar occurrences, all involving reports of positive assurances from the person who had died and an immediate resolution of the traumatic grief. He was completely at a loss to explain why these patients were reporting these experiences – until he looked back over his notes to see if there was any difference in the treatment he had given them. He then noticed that on those occasions he had provided an additional set of eye movements without giving the patient any particular instructions. This sequence seemed to have 'opened' them to the experiences they had had. To test this, Botkin tried the sequence on another patient the next day with the same results: the patient reported that he 'saw' his deceased daughter playing happily, looking healthy and sending him love. Over the next few months Botkin repeated his newly discovered technique with a 98% success rate, despite being shocked each time it happened. He then (with some trepidation) decided to share his experiences with some colleagues, who started to use it with equal success. One remarkable feature of the therapy was that it was found to produce a permanent resolution of the deep-seated problems of the patients, rather than fading over time as hallucinations tend to do.

The use of this technique, now known as IADC (induced after-death communication), has spread over the last 20 years and IADC-trained therapists are now to be found across North America, Europe, India and Africa; a specialist Institute has also been established in Germany. As a healing therapy it seems undeniably to be successful in cases where other approaches are not, but the key question from the perspective of our book is whether the patients' experiences really do reflect a novel method of communicating with the dead without the help of a medium. (Although the therapist could perhaps be seen as a 'medium' of sorts, he or she is not dependent on any psychical gift or power.)

Botkin himself stresses that it is irrelevant what the patient or the therapist believes about the process. Despite describing the technique as induced after-death communication, he is far from dogmatic about how and why it works and what is actually going on. He doesn't, for example, claim that his findings 'prove' life after death, insisting that the crucial point about IADC therapy is that "it works, dramatically, so it is worthy of study and common application in therapy." Yet while fair-mindedly offering a possible naturalistic explanation in terms of some unknown brain mechanism, Botkin and most of his patients clearly favor the more obvious interpretation in terms of direct communication with those who have died. He also has been struck by similarities between IADC experiences and some features of NDEs.

This interpretation is strongly supported by the many fascinating case studies described in his book, where at times accurate information unknown to the patient at the time is communicated, and sometimes the IADC experienced by the patient is even shared by others present. One patient, for example, saw the 'communicator' playing with his sister's dog and only later discovered that the sister had indeed lost a dog similar to the one seen. Another experienced his dead adoptive father apologizing for his coldness towards him as a baby, of which he was unaware but which his mother later confirmed. Another Vietnam veteran experienced his previous commanding officer, whom he thought was still alive, apologizing for his behavior, only to discover afterwards that the man had indeed been killed. On another occasion a trainee therapist observing Botkin's technique experienced the same images that the patient had done. Other therapists reported similar instances of shared IADC experiences. These cases convinced Botkin that IADC experiences could not be explained as hallucinations. Yet if they are not, it seems reasonable to conclude that they represent an important breakthrough in afterlife studies.

The material we've briefly surveyed in this chapter suggests that communication with those who have died may take many different forms and is not necessarily dependent on a medium. Nor is information about a possible afterlife available only from religious authority figures or only available to religious believers. Many thousands of people have now reported NDEs and IADCs, while Dewi Rees's study of bereaved spouses implies that many millions accept that they have been contacted by their former partners, though they may often be reluctant to reveal this. It seems, then, that we don't need to participate in Victorian-style séances or consult a priest in order have such experiences or gain evidence for life after death.

So who can know about a possible afterlife? Perhaps we all can. It's now time to recap on the ground we've covered so far, to try to draw some provisional conclusions, and to work out where we individually stand on these fundamental questions which directly affect the lives and deaths of each one of us.

Conclusions

Chapter 17

So Will We Survive Death?

We've now travelled a long way in our investigation from our starting point in the Introduction with those eight typical responses to the question, "Do you believe in life after death?" and we should be in a better position to reach some reasonable conclusions. Our aim has not been to 'prove' any of those eight responses right or wrong, but to show how we need to recognize that a huge amount of evidence, argument and experience has to be taken into account if we are to form any sort of considered opinion on the matter. Serious questions deserve serious attention, and there can be few more serious questions than those concerning the death and ultimate destiny of ourselves and others. Our response to this question about death, even if we try consciously to ignore it, will inevitably affect our whole outlook on life.

How can we decide what that response should be and whether or not it's reasonable to believe in an afterlife? In the same way that we should approach any important question, by looking as closely as we can at all the relevant information we have access to, by listening to the arguments on all sides and by trying to judge which 'experts' and 'authorities' deserve to be trusted. 'Experts' often disagree, however, and that trust must always be provisional. We'll need to know what those people with specialist knowledge of various kinds can tell us, but that doesn't mean blindly accepting their opinions and judgments without question, whether they be scientists, theologians, spiritualists or atheists. No one can approach any important issue from a position of complete neutrality; everyone will to some extent see that issue through a filter reflecting their individual experiences and assumptions, however unconscious that process may be at times. We're all in the same position as the 'experts' in this respect. We can acquaint ourselves with some of the available evidence about life after death, but our final judgment will always be **our** judgment from **our** perspective and will be partly colored by **our** previous beliefs and experiences.

We'll return to the subject of personal experience at the end of this chapter, but first we must briefly review some of the factors described in this book which we can take into account in deciding our response to the question we've been tackling. To avoid getting too bogged down by the problem of which individual 'experts' and 'authorities' we can trust and which we should avoid, we'll focus more generally on those areas of knowledge and understanding which we've drawn upon in our investigation so far. The two main sources of evidence and argument have come from psychical and religious sources, so let's now revisit these in turn before considering the role of personal experience.

Psychical Sources

We saw in the earlier chapters of this book that the challenge to the Church's monopoly as the sole authority on life after death came originally from two separate directions – from spiritualism and psychical research. These differed in many ways but shared a crucial common factor – mediumship. It was the phenomenon of mediumship that triggered the dramatic spread of spiritualism, and that also provided the target of much of the early investigations into the possibility of survival by psychical researchers.

Examples of the evidence provided by mediums and the controversies it has generated have been described in previous chapters, but it must be emphasized yet again that this represents a tiny fraction of the material available. Some of this evidence has been judged by researchers to be very strong – such as that coming from the cross-correspondences, the R101 case, the Scole studies, and from individual mediums like Mrs. Piper, Mrs. Willett, Geraldine Cummins and Leslie Flint, who were never detected in any kind of fraud. Statistical evidence showing the unlikelihood of mediums' results being achieved by chance has also been produced by university researchers both in America and the UK. These examples should help to dispel the commonly-held assumption that all mediums are fakes or deluded, and never deliver specific, accurate messages to sitters.

Critics have tried to explain away this data by suggesting that mediums may be able to have unlimited access to information stored in the memories of living people and in documentary sources (the so-called 'Super-ESP Theory'), but it has been frequently pointed out that not a shred of evidence exists to support this theory, and that no medium has ever demonstrated extraordinary powers of this kind. Ironically, the theory has sometimes been advocated by arch-skeptics who tend to deny **all** forms of paranormal activity and psychical ability, yet 'Super ESP' would demand the existence of an unheard of degree of paranormal telepathy. The theory seems to have far less empirical support, then, than the idea that individual consciousness may survive physical death.

We've also seen how further compelling evidence has come from psychical sources that don't require the involvement of mediums. These include experiences of 'crisis apparitions', of contact with deceased spouses, of continuing consciousness when clinically 'dead', of communications with deceased persons associated with patients' traumatic grief and of contact with deceased persons by means of electronic equipment.

So how can we assess all this material? However convincing it may seem, we must always remember that 100% guaranteed 'proof' is impossible here, as it is with any complex, controversial question. Skeptics can always try to produce an alternative 'explanation', however implausible, for any individual piece of evidence, but it's the **cumulative** weight of numerous pieces of evidence that creates such a strong case. Some have used the analogy of a bundle of sticks to illustrate this vital point. A single stick can easily be snapped in a way that a thick bundle of sticks cannot. In the same way, a single piece of evidence for survival can always be challenged by attempts to explain it away, but to try to do that for this whole huge mass of data, as some dogmatic materialists try to do, must strain the credulity of any rational person to breaking point.

Religious Sources

It has been impossible to present in a book of this length a comprehensive summary of religious approaches to life after death, as there are so many forms that religion can take and consequently so many sets of belief about an afterlife. For that reason, traditional Christianity has been highlighted as an example of a particular religious perspective which most readers will be familiar with, and one which has often viewed the psychical sources above with suspicion if not outright hostility.

We've seen how the orthodox doctrines of the Christian Church on the subject of life after death have often been confused and confusing, and have for centuries been based on the images of an eternal Heaven for those accepting these doctrines and an eternal Hell for those who reject them. Modern, liberal Christians may be uneasy about these images, but there has been little attempt to develop the Church's overall thinking about an afterlife. The result has been that many clergy seem embarrassed about the whole subject and are reluctant to commit themselves to any clear set of beliefs about it. Very few show any awareness of, or interest in, the psychical evidence we've been exploring. Many people then assume, consciously or unconsciously, either that the Church has nothing helpful now to say about the possibility of life after death, or that its traditional doctrines, with all their unfortunate associations, still represent the official 'party line'. This situation may well be a factor in the steady decline in church membership, attendance and funeral services in recent years.

Should we then dismiss 'religion' as a source of evidence for an afterlife? By no means. Just because one particular form of religion doesn't seem to be able to contribute anything very satisfactory in this respect, that doesn't mean that religious understanding and insights can be ignored *en bloc*.

All the major religious traditions, Eastern and Western, involve a belief in some form of life after death, and that belief seems to go back to the very earliest times we have any record of. This doesn't of course in itself prove anything. Sheer numbers cannot guarantee the truth of any belief, as is shown by the almost universal acceptance for centuries of the idea of a flat earth at the center of the universe. Yet belief in an afterlife is significantly different from this example as it's easy to understand why people held these beliefs about the shape and position of earth – they look as if they are obviously true. Believing that a dead body doesn't necessarily signify the death of the personality who inhabited that body, however, is far from appearing obviously true, and is in fact wholly counterintuitive. The death of a body **looks** on the face of it like the death of the person whose body it was.

Nevertheless, belief in an afterlife is a central feature of all religious traditions (with the possible exception of some strands of Buddhism). The billions of people following these traditions may all have been mistaken, but such a widespread and non-obvious belief in an afterlife cannot be wholly ignored as evidence. Also, any belief in a just and benevolent God seems to require belief in our continued existence in some form after death. A God who is willing indiscriminately to snuff out the lives of billions of his own creatures, sometimes after only a few minutes and often after years of hardship and pain, with no opportunity for further growth and development, can hardly qualify as just or benevolent.

Do the various religious traditions reveal any consensus about an afterlife? We would not expect identical views to emerge from such diverse sources, and considerable diversity is found also within different strands of the same religion, but even a very brief overview reveals some staggering similarities when we consider that they come from so wide a variety of cultures and periods of history. Let's glance at a sample selection. An adequate survey is again way beyond the scope of this book.

Zoroastrianism, for example, one of the world's oldest living religions, goes back probably over 3000 years and still has about a quarter of a million followers. It was the prevailing religion of much of the Near East at the time when Christianity first arose. It teaches that the soul of the departed stays close to the body for three days after death, after which it is guided through a form of judgment towards an environment which may be very pleasant, very unpleasant or neutral, though Light will eventually prevail over darkness. Ancient Egyptian religion also placed great emphasis on moving towards the Light after death, on resurrection and on a judgment of one's conduct, resulting in rewards or punishments.

One basic belief of Hinduism is that each individual has a divine element or seed, which leaves the physical body at death to be united with the Lord, who is the giver of light. This divine seed is described in the key Hindu scripture, the *Bhagavad Gita* (*The Song of God*), as "deathless, birthless, unchanging for ever" and the basis of existence for everything "animate or inanimate".

Judaism has a wide spectrum of beliefs about the afterlife, but there has been general agreement that all souls rise to a higher level after a year in Sheol, which is a state of purgatory where spiritual cleansing can take place before one goes to be with God. Some branches of Judaism also believe in a physical resurrection, when the 'spark of God' will be rekindled and the soul reunited with the physical body.

In Islam, the hereafter begins with the general resurrection of humanity, followed again by a judgment, based on the moral significance of everything one has done and thought and said. Paradise and Hell are vividly described, the former offering a range of sensual delights while the latter resembles a medieval torture chamber. An intermediate state between the two is also pictured, but overall God's forgiveness and mercy will eventually prevail.

These common themes of judgment and returning to some sort of union with God are repeated in other religions, such as those followed by the Baha'i and by Native American Indians. There are obvious parallels here with some Christian beliefs.

Predictably there are some clear differences in the pictures of the afterlife painted by these religious traditions, notably on the subject of reincarnation. However, religious language is essentially a symbolic matter, and we find here striking similarities and overlaps between the symbols, the metaphors and the allegories being used. Even in these brief examples just given, we can notice several common symbols and metaphors. There is the divine spark or seed that is implanted or incarnated within us all and which ensures our immortality; there is the resurrection or reunion of that divine element with God after death; and there is the cleansing or judgmental process that allows us to move on into a realm of Light. Many Christians may be surprised to learn that these themes and the symbols and metaphors used to express them, such as incarnation and resurrection, represent religious insights which predate Christianity by many hundreds, in some cases many thousands, of years.

How might we try to explain these common features, shared by such different traditions? Are they somehow 'hardwired' into our consciousness? Some have argued that such symbols as the cross, the sun and the divine spark within us are all 'archetypes', implanted by God in the deep well of our human unconscious. The notions of 'incarnation' and 'resurrection' have appeared in various forms in the myths and allegories of pre-Christian religions from the earliest times, and were particularly prominent in the so-called Mystery Religions. These developed from ancient Egyptian origins in many civilizations which flourished in the Mediterranean area, and which featured, under different names and mythical forms, a 'godman' who entered our world, identified with us, suffered a sacrificial death before being resurrected, a destiny which followers could all share. Such myths were believed to represent the spiritual journey and experience of us all and the ways in which the human and the divine are enmeshed with each other. The many parallels here with Christianity could hardly be plainer. These have led some scholars to argue that the original form of Christianity was as a Jewish version of these Mystery Religions, and that the name 'Jesus Christ', versions of which had appeared in many other religions, represents symbolically the 'divine spark' implanted in humanity by God, rather than an historical individual (see e.g. Freke and Gandy, 1999). The radical Canadian theologian Tom Harpur (2007) is not alone in suggesting that the whole traditional Christian story should be seen as an allegory for God's gift of that spark to all living creation, not as a literal, biographical account of one unique 'godman'. (Whether this gift and the prospect of an afterlife that it offers is limited to human beings, or whether it might also be shared by some or all nonhuman animals are further fundamental questions beyond the scope of this book, but it's worth noting that some religious traditions attribute much more spiritual significance and sacredness to animals than does Christianity. The idea of animals surviving physical death is also supported by some psychical evidence of apparitions and materializations and by the claims of some mediums to be able to communicate with animals who have died; animals tend to feature frequently in sittings of pet-owners with mediums.)

Another possible, intriguing explanation for some of the common features in religious accounts of an afterlife is that they may have an empirical basis. Some recent researchers have suggested that these images of the afterlife may be derived from actual experiences reported within each religious tradition, including what we now label as NDEs as well as other mystical and psychical experiences. Certainly the religious image of moving towards the Light or towards a Being of Light, which is described in so many modern NDEs, might have arisen from such experiences. Some forms of Buddhism, for example, such as Pure Land Buddhism, have been shown to reflect closely the typical features of NDEs.

Religions, then, can contribute to the evidence for an afterlife, though this is clearly not the kind of evidence that can be tested scientifically. Religious insights are no different in this respect from moral or artistic insights, but that doesn't mean that they have no validity. An important caveat needs to be entered here, however. Our assessments of the evidence for and against the possibility of life after death should not be dominated or dictated by the doctrines and teachings of any one religion. We can't use particular dogmas or creeds to support or reject the evidence or to settle the question. We all know the disastrous results of mixing up religious and scientific arguments, as in the cases of the Church's reaction to Galileo and Darwin.

It's not legitimate, then, in considering the evidence and the arguments about an afterlife to dismiss out of hand all the extensive data on the possibility of reincarnation, for example, just because that may conflict with some (though not all) Christian beliefs; equally, that data cannot be accepted just because it may support some Hindu or Buddhist beliefs. Or to take another example, all the psychical evidence on apparent post-mortem communications and on near-death experiences is not to be ignored simply because it may contradict some traditional Christian doctrines, such as those suggesting that death is followed by a comatose state of lengthy hibernation, lasting until a final Day of Judgment, or that one's fate after death is dependent on the particular religious beliefs (or lack of them) that one may have held during one's life.

There's another problem about accepting only that evidence that accords with the beliefs and doctrines and creeds of a particular religion. Taking again the example of Christianity here, if it is demanded that only that evidence which reflects Christian beliefs is accepted, what precisely would these Christian beliefs be? How exactly is the word 'Christian' to be defined? The same point can be made about the terms 'Buddhist', 'Hindu' and 'Islamic', but if we keep the focus on Christianity, we know that its history has been marked throughout by controversy, power struggles, censorship and conflicts of all kinds, often very violent kinds, which has resulted in a huge diversity of beliefs, practices and doctrines. Estimates vary from between 400 and over 2000 different and often competing Christian denominations and sects. Recent surveys have shown widespread disagreement both within and between a variety of Christian churches on key issues and doctrines such as the Resurrection, salvation, the Virgin Birth, the Trinity, Original Sin, Atonement, the Second Coming, and, crucially for our purposes here, life after death. So what would these 'Christian' beliefs be that the evidence would have to conform to? We've seen in earlier chapters that it seems impossible to identify anything that could be properly called the standard, orthodox 'Christian' view of the afterlife.

Religion then can contribute significantly to the evidence we need to consider, as long as that evidence is not constrained or censored by the doctrinal demands of any one particular religious tradition. Those demands can quickly lead to the tensions that we've explored earlier in this book, when they conflict with evidence from psychical sources. Yet where there is no such conflict, the symbols and insights associated with many religions can **support** that evidence and set it within a broader and richer perspective. The image of an immortal 'divine spark' within us all which will survive the death of our physical bodies, and which will enable us to enjoy a form of 'rebirth' into an environment where our individual experiences and consciousness will continue is completely compatible with much of the psychical evidence; so is the idea that our earthly lives will be appraised and assessed after death in some kind of 'judgment' (whether by 'God' or our 'higher selves'), which will help us to make further spiritual progress.

We should not ignore, then, the light that religions can throw upon the questions about a possible life after death. 'Religion' is not easily defined, however, and as we saw in Chapter 2 an important distinction can be drawn between 'institutional' and 'personal' religion. This distinction points the way to another possible form of evidence for life after death – personal evidence.

The Evidence of Personal Experience

The symbols, myths and allegories shared by many religions described above are a key element in their traditions, practices and teachings. They can in this sense be called 'institutional', though not all of these religions qualify as 'institutions' in the way that Christianity does in having an established structure of organization and doctrine. In Chapter 2 we found that the approach of William James in his classic study of the subject was to "ignore the institutional branch entirely, to say nothing of the ecclesiastical organization, to consider as little as possible the systematic theology and the ideas about the gods themselves, and to confine myself as far as I can to personal religion pure and simple." In this way James was able to study the subject in a way that avoided the common assumption that a person's religion is wholly a matter of his or her attachment to an established religious institution.

Despite declaring that he was unable to accept "popular Christianity", James gives many fascinating and often lengthy accounts of reported experiences of "an altogether other dimension of existence from the sensible and merely 'understandable' world. Name it the mystical region or the supernatural region, whichever you choose... we belong to it in a more intimate sense than that in which we belong to the visible world." How was this region related to a possible afterlife? James did not deal directly with the issues of what he termed "immortality" or "spirit-return", though he noted that for most people "religion *means* immortality" and that he was himself "somewhat impressed by (the) favourable conclusions" of psychical researchers such as Frederic Myers.

James' focus on personal experience anticipated the work more than 50 years later by another academic who dared to combine his scientific, religious and psychical interests, the biologist, Sir Alister Hardy, whom we met in an earlier chapter. In a newspaper article in 1969, which launched a groundbreaking research program, he posed what has become known as 'the Hardy question': "Have you ever been aware of a presence or power which is different from your everyday self?" As a result of the many responses he received, an extensive archive was built up and is still being added to, containing many thousands of accounts of personal experiences. These cover a wide range and include, for example, feeling the presence and guidance of God or of a particular religious figure, feeling 'at one' with Nature, having a prayer answered, perceiving an event without the aid of the five senses, feeling that one has left one's physical body, and sensations of light and overpowering love. It's claimed that perhaps over half the population has had such experiences.

Like William James, Hardy was not concerned directly with the question of life after death in his research, but his collection of personal experiences did include many of a 'psychical' kind, some of which did refer clearly to that subject. One woman, for example, described how after her husband's sudden death she saw and spoke to him and held his hand: "This hand was strong and not at all ghost-like, nor was his appearance." This was one of several experiences that she said proved to her that there is a life after death and that God exists. Another woman reported seeing the apparition of her dead husband, "radiant, smiling, his usual happy self, … completely himself, but of a different 'substance'," an experience that had given her great comfort (Hardy, 1979).

These reports are very similar to those gathered by Dr. Dewi Rees, described in Chapter 16, and to those of so-called 'crisis apparitions'. Evidence from personal experience, then, should not be seen as a separate form of evidence. All of the material referred to in this book is based in some way on such experience. Obviously NDEs are reported personal experiences as are those associated with Botkin's IADCs. Even material produced by mediums involves personal experience – that of the mediums themselves and that of the sitter whose role is to receive and interpret the information.

Why then should we pick out personal experience for special attention here? There are several important reasons for doing so. Firstly, it emphasizes that the search for evidence on this subject is not the monopoly of 'specialists'. You don't have to be a medium or a mystic or a psychical researcher or a cleric in order to have access to this evidence. No special qualifications or expertise is required. Experiences of this kind seem to be relatively common. On the basis of Alister Hardy's research, perhaps half of the population has had experience of a "presence or power different from their everyday self", while the findings of Dewi Rees and others suggest that about the same proportion of bereaved spouses have had "some perception of, or contact with" their dead husbands or wives. Significant numbers of patients have also reported having a near-death experience, while many more will have had some contact with a medium. Evidence relevant to the question of life after death, then, is not available only to an exclusive elite, even though many people are reluctant for various reasons to admit to having had these experiences.

Another reason for highlighting the role of personal experience here is the degree of conviction that it can carry. One can study all the religious arguments for life after death and read all the reports of psychical researchers, and find this mass of data intellectually convincing. Yet a single direct personal experience of the kind we have mentioned can bring with it a level of psychological certainty that secondhand material cannot. It was striking that Oliver Lodge and Conan Doyle began their passionate campaigns to spread the word about psychical evidence for life after death only after they had received what was for them direct confirmation that they had been in contact with deceased family members. Yet both men were already well-acquainted with the extensive body of existing psychical evidence, and Lodge had accepted it as decisive. Bishop Pike's convictions about an afterlife similarly arose from his experiences following the death of his son.

This feature of personal experience was also probably a major factor in the appeal and rapid spread of spiritualism in its early years and in the movement's survival up to the present day. The communications produced by spiritualist mediums were, and still are, intended for specific individuals, who are free to accept or reject them. To receive a message which one judges to come from someone who has died must inevitably be a powerful personal experience, much more so than hearing or reading someone else's report.

The skeptic will at this point probably raise a general objection to the whole idea of seeing personal experience as a valid form of evidence. Don't we all know how easy it is to deceive and delude ourselves, to misinterpret and be mistaken about what we think we are seeing and hearing? Of course we do, but that's not a reason to dismiss personal experience as a form of evidence – after all, all 'evidence', including scientific evidence, is in one sense dependent on such experience and on the interpretation and reporting of it.

We can and should always try to examine and assess our experiences, not just take them at face value. This kind of self-analysis isn't easy to do, but if we are aware of the difficulties, it's not impossible to take a fairly objective view of our experiences and to try to analyze how we interpret them, just as we would someone else's. One great advantage of using one's own personal experience in this way is that one can have much more information about the details and the background than is possible about someone else's experience. Some of the best psychical researchers, past and present, have demonstrated this by being willing to present and examine their own experiences as a source of evidence, as we've seen in the case of Professor David Fontana, for example.

So, as our title asks, who on earth can know anything about the possibility of life after death? The answer is anyone, in short, who is prepared to consider the question seriously enough to have a look at the evidence, which we've seen can come from a number of different sources. Experts in various fields can help us in doing this, but they can never have the last word on the subject or claim to be 'the authority' on the subject. Ultimately, each of us has to make up their own minds, and some may be fortunate enough to be able to add their own personal experience to the package of evidence. The simple response, then, to the question of who can know anything about life after death is **YOU**, the reader!

But what exactly is that question asking? Most of the material we've been looking at has centered on the evidence for whether or not we can and do survive our physical death, and whether or not our consciousness and our personality continue in some form after our bodies and our brains have ceased to function. The answer to these questions must be a straightforward yes or no; either we survive or we don't. This leads to a further question, though, which is far from straightforward and which we've so far said relatively little about. If we decide, however tentatively, that in view of all the evidence it's reasonable to accept provisionally that we do survive physical death, what is that life after death going to be like? Is it possible to know anything about the conditions and environment that make up 'the afterlife'?

Some of the material we've looked at has touched upon this further question. Some religious doctrines have tried to describe what the believer (and nonbeliever) may expect to experience, though in the case of Christianity its teachings have often been contradictory and either so vague as to be meaningless or so specific as to be ridiculous. Some of the psychical evidence of earlier chapters produced by mediums has also involved reports of afterlife conditions; the communications apparently received from Raymond Lodge, for example, did not only aim to establish his survival but also gave details of the world he now found himself in – though his father rightly judged this material to be less "evidential".

In the following final chapter, then, we'll try to tackle this question directly to see whether it makes any sense to think that we can discover anything about what to expect if we do indeed survive our physical deaths.

Chapter 18

What Might the Afterlife Be Like?

Oliver Lodge, with his usual caution, decided that Raymond's descriptions of the afterlife could not provide the same kind of evidence that much of his other communications did. This seems a reasonable judgment. Most of us assume that even if there is a life after death of some kind, it must be necessarily shrouded in mystery and we can know nothing about it. Yet in fact there **does** exist a large number of alleged descriptions of the afterlife which have been given over the years by mystics, mediums and people close to death.

It's quite possible, of course, to dismiss all of these descriptions. Perhaps they are all the result of wishful thinking; perhaps they simply reflect the conscious or subconscious beliefs of the medium or whoever is delivering the description. That may well happen in some cases. But if we don't dismiss out of hand the possibility that **some** of these descriptions may just be what they claim to be, and are prepared to approach these accounts critically but open-mindedly, the question arises how might we try to assess their reliability and judge which ones seem to carry the most weight. This task may appear impossible at first sight because we are handicapped by still living an earthly life, and so have no yardstick to measure the accuracy of afterlife accounts by. Might we still, however, work out some possible tests or indicators that we might use to help us to make some tentative assessments?

If we're faced with an alleged description of the afterlife communicated through a medium, how can we even start to judge whether it is a reliable, independent account from someone who is actually experiencing that afterlife, or whether it's merely a reflection, conscious or unconscious, of the medium's own beliefs and assumptions, as many skeptics maintain?

One test we might try is very similar to one we might use to assess any material communicated through a medium: what sort of checkable evidence is offered by the alleged communicator? There's an obvious problem here. We can't expect verifiable evidence about conditions in the afterlife, because we are not in a position to check that evidence directly. Yet the communicator **can** provide other kinds of evidence about matters that can be checked. So if the communicator offers verifiable information about **this** world, then it's reasonable to suppose that any information about the next world may not be entirely unreliable. In fact, there are many examples of this mixture of information coming from communicators, some of whom we've already met in earlier chapters. This isn't surprising, as a communicator trying to contact and identify themselves to a recipient would be likely also to want to give some idea of the conditions they were experiencing.

However, one form of mediumship has not featured in this book because it often completely lacks this element of verifiable confirmation. This is the phenomenon of 'channeling', which aims not to produce specific evidence of the survival of a particular person after death, but to convey much more general 'spiritual wisdom' and 'inspirational teaching' on a wide range of topics. The apparent communicators here are usually said to be historical characters, sometimes Biblical or associated with some other spiritual tradition, though some prefer to remain nameless; Native Americans are commonly involved, with such names as White Eagle or Silver Birch. The material emanating from channeling, or some of it, may or may not be what it claims to be (who can tell?), but its exclusion from this book is because, if it contains no checkable information, it cannot qualify as 'evidential', to use Oliver Lodge's term again, and so falls outside our scope. Lacking any verifiable support, it is clearly more open to self-deception and to the possible conscious or unconscious influence of the medium.

As we've seen, Lodge and his family received a large amount of convincing evidential material of varying kinds, claiming to come from his son, Raymond, **as well as** detailed descriptions of the afterlife. Rev. Charles Drayton Thomas, a Methodist minister, received extensive communications allegedly from his dead father and sister, containing lots of information about the next world, but also detailed book and newspaper tests which seemed deliberately designed to provide Drayton Thomas with convincing empirical evidence which he could verify. Communications given to Bishop James Pike, apparently from his son who had committed suicide, likewise combined accurate references and predictions of events that would befall his father, together with descriptions of his own post-mortem experiences.

Some examples, including the three mentioned above, also demonstrate another form of evidence – evidence of an enduring, distinctive, recognizable personality, yet one that shows signs of development and enlarged understanding occurring after physical death. The material said to come from Mrs. Coombe-Tennant, transmitted through the writing medium, Geraldine Cummins, also demonstrated considerable character development. Another interesting example was the series of post-mortem messages allegedly communicated by Sir Arthur Conan Doyle (Cooke, 1963). These were often delivered in his own distinctive style and reportedly accompanied by typical mannerisms and gestures, yet they indicated that he had refined and developed some of his thinking about spiritual matters as a result of his recent experiences. As one might expect from one who during his lifetime had placed great emphasis upon the evidence for survival, he prefaced his detailed and comprehensive account of the afterlife with an impressive piece of personal, verifiable evidence. This took the form of an original "spirit photograph" of himself, which he predicted would be communicated, and which was produced by a medium who knew nothing of the prediction or of the sitter's involvement with Conan Doyle.

These kinds of supporting evidence can add some weight and authority to the picture of the afterlife that these people are painting. However, if we are faced, as we are, with a large number of accounts, many of which do offer these kinds of evidence, what further tests can we apply? One possible way forward here is to look for consistency. If we keep finding the same or similar features cropping up in different accounts, that may be significant. When a number of witnesses are in agreement about something, that does not of course provide cast-iron proof (they may all be mistaken, or in league with each other), but it does call for explanation and serious attention.

In fact, we find that there **is** a lot of agreement and consistency between many afterlife accounts. There is considerable agreement, for example, about the actual experience of death and its immediate aftermath. There is also general agreement to a large extent about the overall pattern and structure of afterlife experiences, in terms of a gradual development through a number of what are variously described as stages, levels, spheres or modes of consciousness, though there are variations in the descriptions of the precise sequence and nature of these stages.

The most important studies undertaken in this area must be the groundbreaking research done by Dr. Robert Crookall, which we've described in some detail in Chapter 15. There we saw that his method of collecting and comparing many afterlife accounts revealed a number of striking similarities, such as a life-review and form of 'judgment'. Despite these common features that Crookall uncovered, however, there is still far from total agreement or consistency between afterlife accounts. They often differ in the individual experiences they claim to describe and in the detailed sequence of post-mortem events. Some contain what seems to be very odd and idiosyncratic material.

What are we to make of these apparent discrepancies? Perhaps this mixture of consistency and inconsistency is exactly what we should expect from authentic accounts. If a hundred spaceships from some distant planet were to land at different points on the Earth's surface, and sent back reports of their surroundings and experiences, there would be huge differences in their descriptions (of areas such as the Arctic, a desert or a major city), but also a lot of agreement (e.g. about the general size, shape and structure of the Earth's human inhabitants). In the same way, when afterlife accounts differ, this might simply reflect wide variations in the conditions that are being experienced, depending perhaps on the length of time that has elapsed since the person's death, the character of that person and the progress and development (or lack of it) that may have occurred.

We might also logically expect to find more consistency and agreement about **immediate** after-death experiences than about later ones. If a group of your friends were to fly to a foreign country and then set off on individual explorations in different directions, sending you back postcards as they went, you would expect any postcards sent from the airport to contain much more uniform information than those sent a week or a month later. Again, this is very much what we find with the information allegedly received about the afterlife – the 'airport postcards' are the most consistent and predictable.

Yet some of the inconsistencies and oddities may be as significant as the similarities. The descriptions apparently given by Raymond Lodge were ridiculed by some critics when he told of his fellow soldiers being provided with cigars and whisky sodas on arrival. Another after-death communicator, Helen Salter, a former prominent member of the SPR, tells of finding a replica of her childhood home waiting for her. Others seem to spend some of their time on what we might call spiritual tourism, visiting all sorts of exotic locations on the earth and even in outer space. The former nun and influential early member of the CFPSS, Frances Banks, speaks of working in a Rest Home run by the Sisters of her religious Order, and of going on rescue missions to the lower gloomy regions of the 'Shadow Lands' (Greaves, 1969).

What are we to make of these strange reports? The first point to recognize is that we should be very suspicious if there was total agreement between the various accounts. That could well suggest that the mediums or recipients of this material were consciously or unconsciously following some psychic or spiritual 'party line' and regurgitating details they had heard or read elsewhere. Incidentally, that possibility is why this is one area of research where we can place more weight upon earlier data (such as Raymond Lodge's communications) rather than recent material, which is much more likely to have been influenced by what has gone before. A similar point can be made about reports of NDEs, where the earliest accounts will not have been influenced by the mass of material which has accumulated more recently.

The second point to make is that most of the apparent inconsistencies and oddities can perhaps be explained by one important feature of the earlier stages of the afterlife which many communicators do agree on. The environment in which most people seem to find themselves soon after death is said to be largely mentally created – a world that is in a sense illusory to some extent, made up of material that is described as 'ideoplastic' and 'malleable'. All the things one encounters, according to some communicators, are really thought forms, so arranged as to make the transition easy from material to spirit life. This would mean that the immediate afterlife is partly constructed by our expectations and wish-fulfilment, which can continue until we tire of what Myers called 'Lotus-land' and are ready for something more challenging. One communicator even reported that he had opportunities to play golf in the afterlife, but that he didn't seem to enjoy it as much as he used to. This is strikingly similar to Raymond Lodge's cigar-smoking, whisky-swigging colleagues, whose tastes soon appear to change: "They don't seem to get the same satisfaction out of it. They don't seem to want it so much."

If this really is the immediate post-mortem experience of most people, it raises some fascinating and difficult questions about subjectivity and objectivity in both this world and the next, but it does also explain many, if not all, of the variations and apparently eccentric details in the accounts. "The unthinking man," says the communicator claiming to be our old friend Frederic Myers (rather condescendingly), "will create a glorified brick villa in a glorified Brighton." In fact, some of the quirky, unexpected, way-out items can carry more conviction than the more predictable material. Who, for instance, is likely to make up the report of a former dog-owner, claiming that she is teaching her pet how to 'think food' and create a dishful of his favorite meat?

Are there any further tests we might apply to alleged afterlife descriptions? One final one relates to the nature of religious experience. If any afterlife accounts are really what they claim to be, surely they will be, almost by definition, reports of religious or spiritual experiences. However, we've seen that an extensive database of such experiences already exists, initiated by Sir Alister Hardy, reported by people who have not yet died. William James also includes many such accounts in his book, *The Varieties of Religious Experience*. So if reports allegedly from the next world reflect or agree in some respects with reports from this world, that again would seem to provide some confirmation and support; and again this is what we often find.

Afterlife accounts, for example, speak of experiences of unity and at-one-ment with the world of Nature, with fellow human beings and with God, often in very similar terms to those used in descriptions by people still living. Both types of account refer to experiences of radiance and golden light. Both types of account report feelings of spontaneous joy, uplift and illumination, of sudden insight and understanding – a feeling that everything has meaning and that all shall be well.

There are many examples that could be given of this correspondence between the two types of account, and again Dr. Robert Crookall has done pioneering work here in his book, *The Interpretation of Cosmic and Mystical Experiences* (1969). Jane Sherwood's communicator, 'Scott', for instance, gives this afterlife description: "This was no earthly beauty. There was a 'light' on things and a 'light' in them. Grass, trees and flowers were lighted inwardly by their own beauty. The air itself was light... A shimmering radiance abides continually over all the beauty of field and woodland." This is paralleled by many of the Religious Experience Research Centre's archive reports, for example: "The old church was, I saw, outlined by a stream of golden light. Looking inland I saw every hedge giving off golden flames, quivering." Or again we find the Rev. Drayton Thomas being told by his father and sister, "Remember how, sometimes unexpectedly, you are touched with sudden happiness, an extraordinary uplift, illumination and hope... It is a taste of the feeling which we have all the time." This echoes the kind of earthly experience that Rev. Leslie Weatherhead reported, sitting in a railway carriage: "The great moment came... The whole compartment was filled with light... I never felt more exalted. I felt that all was well with mankind. An indescribable joy possessed me." (Hardy, 1979) This kind of correspondence between accounts of the afterlife and of earthly religious experience, then, must add some weight to both if we use it as possible evidence.

Accounts of the afterlife, then, need not be, as is often supposed, a no-go area as far as critical assessment is concerned. It does seem possible to apply certain tests to such accounts and to make some tentative, rational judgments about them. Of course, we shall all have to wait and see (or not see!) which if any of the many accounts are authentic. These tests for validity should not be viewed as rigid requirements or as necessary conditions, but merely as possible indicators to be used when assessing an account of this kind. The absence of any of these indicators does not necessarily mean that a particular account should be rejected, but the presence of one or more indicator can add significantly to that account's credibility.

What about the role of religion here in assessing alleged descriptions of a life after death? Again much depends on how we interpret that word 'religion'. We've just seen that where a particular description resembles some features of reported earthly religious experiences, that can add some weight to its credibility. That, however, is very different from demanding that, to be acceptable, such descriptions must conform to doctrines about the nature of the afterlife, held by any single religion. Afterlife accounts are not restricted to a single religious tradition, and we've seen in earlier chapters how, even within a single tradition such as Christianity, it would be impossible to agree on what the accepted orthodox teaching about the nature of the afterlife really is.

Despite the insistence from some quarters that religious doctrine is the only valid source of information about the afterlife and that acceptance of that doctrine is the only route to that afterlife, this is not supported by the evidence from apparent actual accounts of experiences, as described above. One of the striking points of agreement between many of the accounts is that the particular content of a person's religious beliefs (or lack of them) is irrelevant to his or her position and progress after death. One main obstacle to that progress is said to be a closed mind, rigidity of thought and inflexible adherence to doctrine and dogma, both of which are conspicuous by their absence in afterlife accounts.

The unimportance of specific religious beliefs and creeds is emphasized even by some communicators who had been immersed in institutional religion during their lifetime and had themselves held firm religious beliefs when alive. The Catholic priest, Monsignor Robert Benson, for example, claims, "I could see volumes of orthodox teachings, creeds and doctrines melting away, because they are not true." (Borgia, 1966) Frances Banks, the former Anglican nun, similarly declares, "There are no tenets, no creeds, no formulae, no hard and fast rules devised by any mind to restrict or confine progress here... No soul is coerced, forced or bound by creeds." (Greaves, 1969) So much, then, for religious orthodoxy!

A mountain of material, therefore, has accumulated over the years, not only providing evidence of the survival of particular individuals after death, but also offering possible glimpses of the conditions they have been experiencing. What those glimpses suggest is obviously less 'evidential' (to use Lodge's term) than information about individual survival, which can often be verifiable. Nevertheless, descriptions of the afterlife should not be written off as worthless fantasies which it's impossible to assess in any way.

So if we do survive death, what is it reasonable to expect? Let's try to summarize very briefly some of the main points of agreement we've found between afterlife reports which satisfy all or most of our suggested test conditions.

Many people soon after death seem to go through a short period of rest or sleep in a rather shadowy, dream-like environment, sometimes described as Hades. This isn't necessarily an unpleasant experience – Myers calls it "a place of half-lights and drowsy peace" – and according to Crookall, it typically lasts about three days. Following this are those stages which are said to be largely mentally created and shaped by the character and desires of the individual. As the communicator claiming to be Conan Doyle puts it, "All depends on the man's mentality and spiritual development at the time of his release... A man does not fall into a honeypot when he passes from earth to the spirit world... Every step towards salvation must be earned." (Cooke, 1963) The lowest of these levels, sometimes called Shadowland or the lower astral region, is often described as a barren, dark, cold, foggy world, reserved for those who have shown no human warmth or compassion during their lifetimes. (It's possibly this area that is glimpsed in some 'negative' NDEs.) The mental attitude of those dwelling in this region in some way creates the place they inhabit until they start to make some spiritual progress towards the light, which is always available. Most people, though, seem to find themselves in 'Summerland' – a world where we can apparently create any environment or experience we like and continue to enjoy it as long as we want to – until we become bored and dissatisfied with this mode of being and wish to move on.

But move on to what? What are some of the steps on this long journey? Most accounts speak of a 'judgment' of some kind, though they don't agree over exactly which stage this occurs at. Some speak of two or even three judgments, the first taking place very soon after death. This isn't a once-and-for-all final, decisive event as many religions picture it, but an educative process whereby we are introduced to a sort of panorama of every outer and inner event of our past life, which includes the thoughts and feelings which our actions have caused other people to have. This can be a long, complex and at times painful business, but it is said to be necessary before further progress can be made. That progress later leads to what is sometimes called the Second Death. This stage is said to be where we choose to shed a large part of our personality, our personal self, in order to find our real individuality. Frederic Myers describes it as "shaking off any dogma, any special outlook which has shaped our mentality, which confines it so that our vision is limited." This could include inflexible religious views, and there are some examples of communicators who seem 'stuck' as a result of their dogmatic beliefs.

After this Second Death, then what? This is where the communicators clearly have to struggle even more to convey anything comprehensible. Various higher stages, spheres or levels are spoken of, leading to that state of unity or at-one-ment which mystics from many spiritual traditions have tried to describe; but the one thing that seems clear about this state is that it's **in**describable. Some accounts put emphasis on the rather mysterious idea of Group Souls. They stress that progress in the afterlife is not a solitary enterprise, but that we are (and perhaps always have been) members of a group, or possibly more than one group, that has its own spiritual identity which everyone contributes to and shares in. These groups may have a leader, but they progress always at the pace of the slowest member.

Finally, what about reincarnation? This is, of course, a vast and controversial subject in its own right, and one that we've barely touched upon, as a proper investigation would lie beyond the scope of this book (see e.g. Stemman, 2012). A recent survey of mediums shows that they are divided in their views, as are the main religious traditions, but some form of reincarnation does seem to be accepted by many communicators, though there is a lot of ignorance and uncertainty about the details. Some have suggested that this may be because of different communicators being on different rungs of the spiritual ladder. We clearly shouldn't expect to get instant enlightenment about everything just by dying.

This book has been all about the wide range of evidence about a possible afterlife that is available to anyone who is prepared to look at it; but it has been constantly emphasized that evidence is not to be equated with proof or certain knowledge. Evidence always has to be for or against something, and it doesn't always lead to an obvious conclusion. Many detective stories involve a piece of evidence which is taken by some (usually the dim policeman) to point in one clear direction, but which turns out to do the reverse. Evidence is never neutral; it always has to be interpreted and assessed by individual observers and investigators.

My aim throughout has been to place you, the reader, in a position where you can make up your own mind about the all-important questions we've been tackling. You don't need to be a medium or a minister, a spiritualist or a parapsychologist, to do this; you don't need to be an expert or specialist of any kind, just as the members of a jury don't have to be experts or specialists on the evidence they have put before them, and on which they have to pass a reasonable verdict. All that is needed is a readiness to consider that evidence in as open-minded and rational a way as possible. We can't expect guaranteed certainty on this, or indeed on anything. The one thing we can be pretty sure of is that whenever we believe we have the whole truth, we probably don't.

On that note, let's give the last word to a man who has played an important part in this book by providing us with some of the best evidence for individual survival of death, the former Prime Minister, Arthur Balfour, through the moving story of his lifelong love of Mary Lyttleton, his 'Palm Sunday Maiden', which we recounted in Chapter 11. Balfour was a poet and philosopher as well as a statesman, and these memorable lines of his serve as a gentle warning to all who believe that they have a sure, unquestionable grasp of 'the truth':

Our highest truths are but half-truths,
Think not to settle down for ever in any truth,
Make use of it as a tent in which to spend a Summer's night,
But build no house of it, or it will be your tomb.

I wish all readers a pleasant summer's night in their tent with this book!

Author Biography

Roger Straughan, MA, PhD has spent his career teaching in schools, colleges and universities, culminating in his holding the post of Reader in Education at the University of Reading, UK. His university research has led to the writing and editing of many books and articles on issues in education, philosophy and ethics, and he has given invited papers at many international conferences. Psychical questions have also been a lifelong interest, and he is an active member of a number of societies and organizations concerned with psychical and spiritual matters. He has been invited to speak at major conferences and has written extensively on these subjects. He is also an authority on the life and works of Sir Arthur Conan Doyle.

Previous Related Title

A Study in Survival: Conan Doyle Solves the Final Problem
(O-Books, ISBN: 978-1-84694-240-2)

Here is dramatic new evidence for the survival of our individual personalities after death. Providing this is an astonishing series of recent communications from a man who died in 1930 and whose mission, when alive, was to bring just such evidence to the notice of the widest possible audience – Sir Arthur Conan Doyle. This study in survival describes in vivid detail the intriguing twists and turns of an investigation worthy of the immortal Sherlock Holmes himself, whose legendary return from apparent death uncannily foreshadows that of his famous creator. The novel and ingenious method of communication and actual content of many of the messages are shown to be characteristic of Sir Arthur, reflecting his colorful personality, and demonstrating paranormal knowledge of major news events. Evidence steadily mounts with Conan Doyle's last surviving direct descendant revealing hitherto undisclosed information and playing a vital role in the unfolding story. This has been described as:

"a fascinating book" – Professor David Fontana

"an intriguing good read" – Professor Archie Roy

"this remarkable and challenging book" – Professor Gary Schwartz

"one of the most fascinating books bearing on the survival question to be published in the last 10 years" – David Lorimer, Scientific and Medical Network

References

Armstrong, Karen (1993). *A History of God*. London: Heinemann.

Barham, Allan (1973). "The Nature of Life after Death", in *Life, Death and Psychical Research*, eds. Pearce-Higgins, J.D. and Whitby, G.S. London: Rider.

Biondi, Massimo (2013). "Spiritualism in Italy: The Opposition of the Catholic Church", in *The Spiritualist Movement: Speaking with the Dead in America and Around the World, vol. 1*, ed. Moreman, Christopher. Santa Barbara, CA: Praeger.

Blum, Deborah (2007). *Ghost Hunters*. London: Century.

Borgia, Anthony (1970). *Life in the World Unseen*. London: Corgi.

Botkin, Allan L. (2005). *Induced After Death Communication*. Charlottesville: Hampton Roads.

Broad, C.D. (1953). *Religion, Philosophy and Psychical Research*. London: Routledge.

Bunce, Barbara (1993). *So Many Witnesses*. Louth: CFPSS.

Carr, John Dickson (1949). *The Life of Sir Arthur Conan Doyle*. London: John Murray.

Carrington, Hereward (1920). *Psychical Phenomena and the War*. New York: American Universities Publishing Company.

Cooke, Ivan (1963). *The Return of Arthur Conan Doyle*. Liss: White Eagle Publishing Trust.

Crookall, Robert (1961). *The Supreme Adventure*. Cambridge: James Clarke.

Crookall, Robert (1965). *Intimations of Immortality*. London: James Clarke.

Crookall, Robert (1966). *The Next World – and the Next*. London: Theosophical Publishing House.

Crookall, Robert (1969). *The Interpretation of Cosmic and Mystical Experiences*. London: James Clarke.

Cummins, Geraldine (1965). *Swan on a Black Sea*. London: Routledge.

Dawkins, Richard (2006). *The God Delusion*. London: Bantam.

Doyle, Arthur Conan (1918). *The New Revelation*. London: Hodder & Stoughton.

Doyle, Arthur Conan (1920). *Our Reply to the Cleric*. Halifax: Spiritualists' National Union.

Doyle, Arthur Conan (1926). *The History of Spiritualism*. London: Psychic Press.

Flint, Leslie (1971). *Voices in the Dark*. London: Two Worlds.

Fontana, David (1995). *Is There an Afterlife?* Ropley: O-Books.

Freke, Timothy & Gandy, Peter (1999). *The Jesus Mysteries*. London: Thorsons.

Fuller, John G. (1979). *The Airmen Who Would Not Die*. London: Corgi.

Greaves, Helen (1969). *Testimony of Light*. Saffron Walden: Neville Spearman.

Hamilton, Trevor (2017). *Arthur Balfour's Ghosts*. Exeter: Imprint Academic.

Hardy, Alister (1979). *The Spiritual Nature of Man*. Oxford: Oxford University Press.

Harpur, Tom (1996). *The Thinking Person's Guide to God*. Rocklin, CA: Prima.

Harpur, Tom (2007). *Water Into Wine*. Toronto: Thomas Allen.

Hick, John (1985). *Death and Eternal Life*. Basingstoke: Macmillan.

Holmes, Oliver Wendell (1860). *The Professor at the Breakfast-Table*. Boston: Ticknor and Fields.

Israel, Martin (1993). *Life Eternal*. London: SPCK.

James, William (1960). *The Varieties of Religious Experience*. Glasgow: Collins.

Johnson, Raynor C. (1957). *Nurslings of Immortality*. London: Hodder & Stoughton.

Kollar, Rene (2000). *Searching for Raymond: Anglicanism, Spiritualism, and Bereavement between the Two World Wars*. Lanham, MD: Lexington.

Lester, Reginald M. (1952). *In Search of the Hereafter*. London:

Harrap.

Lodge, Oliver J. (1909). *Survival of Man*. New York: Moffat, Yard.

Lodge, Oliver J. (1916). *Raymond, or Life and Death*. London: Methuen.

Myers, F.W. (1903). *Human Personality and its Survival of Bodily Death*. London: Longmans, Green.

Owen, David (undated). *When the Angel Says Write*. London: Headquarters Publishing.

Perry, Michael (1984). *Psychic Studies*. Wellingborough: Aquarian Press.

Perry, Michael (1992). *Gods Within*. London: SPCK.

Perry, Michael, ed. (1999). *Spiritualism: the 1939 Report to the Archbishop of Canterbury*. Louth: CFPSS.

Perry, Michael (2003). *Psychical and Spiritual*. Louth: CFPSS.

Pike, James A. (1964). *A Time for Christian Candor*. New York: Harper & Row.

Pike, James A. (1967). *If This Be Heresy*. New York: Harper & Row.

Pike, James A. (1969). *The Other Side*. London: W.H. Allen.

Randall, Neville (1975). *Life After Death*. London: Robert Hale.

Rees, Dewi (2010). *Pointers to Eternity*. Talybont: Y Lolfa.

Roy, Archie E. (1996). *The Archives of the Mind*. Stansted: SNU.

Roy, A. and Robertson, T. (2001). "A double-blind procedure for assessing the relevance of a medium's statements to a recipient." *Journal of the Society for Psychical Research*, 65.3, pp. 161-174.

Schwarz, Gary E. (2002). *The Afterlife Experiments*. New York: Atria.

Society for Psychical Research (1999). *The Scole Report*. London: SPR.

Solomon, Grant and Solomon, Jane (1999). *The Scole Experiment*. London: Piatkus.

Stemman, Roy (2012). *The Big Book of Reincarnation*. San Antonio: Hierophant.

Temple, William (1935). *Nature, Man and God*. London: Macmillan.

Twigg, Ena and Brod, Ruth Hagy (1973). *Ena Twigg: Medium*. London: W.H. Allen.

Whitby, Roger (2015). *Gateway*. Psychic Book Club (online).

Williams, H.A. (1982). *Some Day I'll Find You*. London: Mitchell Beazley.

Wingett, Matt (2016). *Conan Doyle and the Mysterious World of Light*. Life is Amazing (online).

Further Reading

The above references give a limited idea of the vast amount of specialist material available on some of the topics covered in this book and can be followed up for further details on those. For readers wishing to go further, the following short list can be recommended to provide general recent overviews of the subject. In alphabetical order:

Betty, Stafford (2016). *When Did You Ever Become Less By Dying?* Hove: White Crow.

Fontana, David (1995). *Is There an Afterlife?* Ropley: O-Books.

Robertson, Tricia (2020). *It's Life and Death, But Not As You Know It!* Hove: White Crow.

Tymn, Michael (2021). *No One Really Dies: 25 Reasons to Believe in an Afterlife*. Hove: White Crow.

Zammit, Victor and Wendy (2013). *A Lawyer Presents the Evidence for the Afterlife*. Hove: White Crow.

6TH
BOOKS

ALL THINGS PARANORMAL

Investigations, explanations and deliberations on the paranormal,
supernatural, explainable or unexplainable. 6th Books seeks to
give answers while nourishing the soul: whether making use of the
scientific model or anecdotal and fun, but always
beautifully written.
Titles cover everything within parapsychology: how to, lifestyles,
alternative medicine, beliefs, myths and theories.
If you have enjoyed this book, why not tell other readers by
posting a review on your preferred book site?

Recent bestsellers from 6th Books are:

The Afterlife Unveiled
What the Dead Are Telling us About Their World!
Stafford Betty
What happens after we die? Spirits speaking through mediums
know, and they want us to know. This book unveils their world...
Paperback: 978-1-84694-496-3 ebook: 978-1-84694-926-5

Spirit Release
Sue Allen
A guide to psychic attack, curses, witchcraft, spirit attachment,
possession, soul retrieval, haunting, deliverance, exorcism and
more, as taught at the College of Psychic Studies.
Paperback: 978-1-84694-033-0 ebook: 978-1-84694-651-6

I'm Still With You
True Stories of Healing Grief Through Spirit Communication
Carole J. Obley
A series of after-death spirit communications which uplift, comfort
and heal, and show how love helps us grieve.
Paperback: 978-1-84694-107-8 ebook: 978-1-84694-639-4

Less Incomplete
A Guide to Experiencing the Human Condition Beyond the
Physical Body
Sandie Gustus
Based on 40 years of scientific research, this book is a dynamic
guide to understanding life beyond the physical body.
Paperback: 978-1-84694-351-5 ebook: 978-1-84694-892-3

Advanced Psychic Development
Becky Walsh
Learn how to practise as a professional, contemporary spiritual
medium.
Paperback: 978-1-84694-062-0 ebook: 978-1-78099-941-8

Astral Projection Made Easy
and overcoming the fear of death
Stephanie June Sorrell
From the popular Made Easy series, *Astral Projection Made Easy*
helps to eliminate the fear of death, through discussion of life
beyond the physical body.
Paperback: 978-1-84694-611-0 ebook: 978-1-78099-225-9

The Miracle Workers Handbook
Seven Levels of Power and Manifestation of the Virgin Mary
Sherrie Dillard
Learn how to invoke the Virgin Mary's presence, communicate
with her, receive her grace and miracles and become a miracle
worker.
Paperback: 978-1-84694-920-3 ebook: 978-1-84694-921-0

Divine Guidance
The Answers You Need to Make Miracles
Stephanie J. King
Ask any question and the answer will be presented, like a direct
line to higher realms... *Divine Guidance* helps you to regain
control over your own journey through life.
Paperback: 978-1-78099-794-0 ebook: 978-1-78099-793-3

The End of Death
How Near-Death Experiences Prove the Afterlife
Admir Serrano
A compelling examination of the phenomena of Near-Death
Experiences.
Paperback: 978-1-78279-233-8 ebook: 978-1-78279-232-1

Readers of ebooks can buy or view any of these bestsellers by
clicking on the live link in the title. Most titles are published
in paperback and as an ebook. Paperbacks are available in
traditional bookshops. Both print and ebook formats are available
online.
Find more titles and sign up to our readers' newsletter at
http://www.johnhuntpublishing.com/mind-body-spirit.
Follow us on Facebook at https://www.facebook.com/OBooks
and Twitter at https://twitter.com/obooks.